UFOs:
12 Things Everyone
Should Know

A CHRISTIAN PERSPECTIVE

Dr. Bobby Brewer

TRILOGY CHRISTIAN PUBLISHERS

Tustin, CA

Trilogy Christian Publishers
A Wholly Owned Subsidiary of Trinity Broadcasting Network
2442 Michelle Drive
Tustin, CA 92780

UFOs: 12 Things Everyone Should Know, A Christian Perspective

For information, address Trilogy Christian Publishing

Rights Department, 2442 Michelle Drive, Tustin, Ca 92780.

Trilogy Christian Publishing/ TBN and colophon are trademarks of Trinity Broadcasting Network.

For information about special discounts for bulk purchases, please contact Trilogy Christian Publishing.

Manufactured in the United States of America.

10 9 8 7 6 5 4 3 2 1

Library of Congress Cataloging-in-Publication Data is available.

ISBN 978-1-68556-769-9

ISBN 978-1-68556-770-5 (ebook)

Endorsements

In *UFO's: 12 Things Everyone Should Know*, Dr. Brewer does a fabulous job of discarding the hearsay, focusing on the facts, and engaging this topic from a Biblical Worldview. I highly recommend this book to anyone who wants to put content to their curiosity about the UFO phenomenon.

—Dr. Joshua Anderson,
Dean of Students, Phoenix Seminary

With credible research from the scientific community, media, the Bible, and other religious texts, Dr. Brewer provides thought-provoking insights into some of the greatest mysteries of our time. His grasp on synthesizing elements and information into a realistic premise for things unexplained will open the reader's mind to evaluative commentary that will allow anyone to draw their own more informed conclusions about this phenomenon and its social, political, anthropological, and religious implications within a Christian worldview.

—Todd Forrest,
Professor of New Testament, Grand Canyon University

Well researched and thoughtfully written, Dr. Bobby Brewer brings a compelling book about aliens, God, and Satan. What was once considered fringe is now mainstream, and you will understand why in *UFO's: 12 Things Everyone Should Know*.

—Dr. Jason Fritz,
Lead Pastor, Illuminate Community Church,
Scottsdale, Arizona

It's easy to go down a rabbit hole on the topic of aliens, but Dr. Brewer guides you down an objective and biblical path. I highly recommend this book!

—Austin Lind,
Missionary, Youth with a Mission (YWAM)

Acknowledgements

"Every time I think of you, I give thanks to my God."
(Philippians 1:3 NLT)

In addition to my wife, Kristen, who supported the purpose and time needed for this book, it wouldn't have been possible without the support of Mariano and Stella Allende, Tim and Lisa Bauer, Bob Hager, Kathy Barnes, Russell and Christina Bilbrey, Darlene Cleaver, Donna Corbin, Todd Forrest, Paul Fredericks, Deanna Grabill, Frank and Glory Hardman, Doug and Stephanie Hay, Kevin and Chantelle Lintini, Shawn and Julie Meneely, Rick and Candy Miller, Lindsay Pisani, Rev. Tim and Tina Stevens, Teresa Parker, and Michael and Kristin Whitchurch.

Special Thanks to:
Nick Pope, Travis Walton, and Shane Hurd (MUFON)

Contents

Introduction

*from Issachar, men who understood the times and
knew what Israel should do...*

(1 Chronicles 12:32 NIV)

Shortly after the publication of Charles Darwin's
Origin of the Species in 1859, a new ideology was clan-
destinely born into mainstream academia. Although
many initially scoffed at Darwin's theory of evolution, it
is hardly a laughing matter today and is still presumed
as an established fact by most people in the Western
world. Initially, Christianity did not consider Darwinism a pertinent issue, but it experienced the proverbial
snowball effect throughout Western civilization because of its acceptance in the academic community. The
Church was caught off guard, and consequently, evolution gained ground without much of a fight and has
continued to gain mainstream acceptance. As a result,
within academia, Christianity was pushed further into
the category of irrelevancy and viewed as superstitious,

archaic, and outdated. The chasm became so wide that even today, some insist on a complete separation between science and spirituality.

Just a decade ago, it felt incredibly awkward to discuss the subject intelligently, and even today, I have no aspirations to be known as the "UFO guy," but I firmly believe that we are in the midst of another philosophical avalanche, and as was the case with Darwinism, the majority of Christians are unprepared. In the early 21st century, the UFO phenomenon solicits the same bemusement from most Christians as evolution did in the late 19th century, but few are laughing about Darwinism today. Consider conducting the following experiment: Ask those in your Bible study if they believe in UFOs. As a follow-up, ask if any have ever actually seen one. More than likely, you'll be surprised at the positive responses you receive to both questions within the Church. For those outside the Church, the UFO phenomenon has already become mainstream and culturally acceptable. In my opinion, it has the same potential to influence the 21st century worldview as Origin of Species, introduced in the 19th century.

As a long-time resident of Arizona, UFOs regularly seem to show up on both the cultural and physical radar. It's next to impossible to visit Sedona without seeing an alien figurine adorning a New Age gift shop. A film, *Fire in the Sky*, was based upon the abduction experience of a resident of Snowflake, and of course, there was the *Phoenix Lights* incident of 1997 that had the whole city asking, "Did you see that last night? What was it?" For the first time, I was being asked what the implications of extraterrestrials visiting earth would have for humanity, religion, and specifically Christianity. Does Christianity have an answer? Should the Christian community even bother to address the presumably preposterous yet pressing issue? What should a parent teach their child about aliens? How can our youth workers answer the E.T. questions of their teenage congregations? And how can you capably address this topic with your friends and family?

After becoming King, David was blessed with a vast array of mighty men and leaders from all twelve tribes. Some were experts in various forms of warfare, but in 1 Chronicles, we're introduced to the "men of Issachar," whom we're told "...understood the times and knew what Israel should do" (1 Chronicles 12:32 NIV). The purpose of this book is that you'll better understand the times and know what to do. As ludicrous as this topic may sound to some, the recognition and acknowledgment of it as a cultural and spiritual phenomenon is essential for effectively ministering to the postmodern culture we now live in, and I commend you for taking the time to understand these times. I believe you'll be wiser for doing so. This is not to suggest we should patronize views about extraterrestrials we do not share. Rather, somewhat like a missionary, we should learn about this "culture" and treat people with the respect they deserve as those created in the image of God who are seeking answers (1 Peter 3:15) and grant this topic its due diligence (Proverbs 25:2).

Before continuing, I should point out that although my views are biblically based, they're not reflective of all evangelical Christians, nor have I received any special prophetic revelation on the topic. My insights and predictions are based on biblical theology and research. Secondly, the UFO phenomenon is somewhat of a rabbit hole that can never be completely exhausted, but the following is an overview of some of its more overarching aspects.

It is my prayer that you will find this volume useful in addressing some of the more pertinent questions regarding this topic and that it will help broaden your understanding of today's postmodern culture. Ideally, this book will aid you in understanding the bigger picture while simultaneously equipping you with more confidence for sharing the gospel with those who speak UFO. May God richly bless you as you seek to become a student of our culture and an ambassador for Jesus Christ for such a time as this.

CHAPTER 1

UFOs Will Become More Mainstream

Most people catch their presupposition from their family and surrounding society the way a child catches measles. But people with more understanding realize that their presuppositions should be chosen after a more careful consideration of what worldview is true.

—Frances Schaeffer

In his book *Messengers of Deception: UFO Contacts and Cults*, Ufologist Jacques Vallee said, "Belief in the reality of UFOs is spreading so rapidly at all levels of society throughout the world. Books and periodicals on the subject appear at an ever-increasing rate. Documentaries and major films are being made now by young people of the UFO generation."[1] UFO researcher J. Allen

---

1 Jacques Valle, *Messengers of Deception: UFO Contacts and Cults* (Berkeley: And/Or Press, 1979), 9.

Hynek, who quite possibly has objectively logged more hours than anyone else in regards to investigating UFOs, said, "As I look back over my past twenty one years association with the UFO problem, I note that the intellectual climate today is enormously better for taking a good look at it than it was even a few years ago."[2] Both of these quotes are from the 20th, not the 21st century. Personalities as diverse as General Douglas MacArthur and British journalist Malcolm Muggeridge have expressed their belief in the existence of Extraterrestrial Intelligence (ETI), a term used to describe beings on other planets who, like us, can manufacture spacecraft, etc. The National Press Club, an organization for journalists and communications professionals, somewhat put its reputation on the line in 2001 when they recruited a vast array of respected government, military, aerospace, and airline personalities who came together to discuss their encounters and beliefs regarding UFOs. The fact that they chose to take the topic seriously gave the phenomenon some credibility. Likewise, on May 17, 2022, a sub-committee in the House of Representatives held a congressional hearing on the topic of UFOs.

"There are a lot of unexplained aerial phenomena. We don't know what they are, and

---

2 Carl Sagan and Thornton Page, American Association for the Advancement of Science, *UFO's: A Scientific Debate* (New York City: Barnes Noble Books, 1996), 50.

they can't be easily rationalized as weather phenomenon or balloons or anything else. So, it's quite a mystery," said House Intelligence Committee Chairman Adam Schiff, D-Calif.[3]

It wasn't that long ago that confession to a belief in aliens would possibly cost your reputation or even call into question your sanity, but today such a belief may qualify you for a research grant.

In 2021, the U.S. Government confirmed that unlike *Project Blue Book* (a study of UFOs by the U.S. Air Force that investigated and provided explanations for most UFO reports from 1952 to 1969), they were *unable* to explain the majority (143 of 144) of aerial phenomena encounters specifically with the military, a complete reversal from *Project Blue Book*'s briefing a half-century earlier.[4] This reflects a paradigm shift from the previous party line in which the U.S. military was generally dismissive of UFOs. Initiated in 1947, quite likely as a result of the Roswell Incident, *Project Sign* was a formal investigation into UFO phenomena conducted by

3 Tyler Olson, "Congress Holds Historic Public UFO Hearing, as Military Struggles to Understand 'mystery' Flying Phenomena," FOX News Network, LLC., 2022, https://www.foxnews.com/politics/house-intelligence-committee-ufo-hearing.

4 Courtney Kube and Adam Edelman, "UFO Report: Government Can't Explain 143 of 144 Mysterious Flying Objects, Blames Limited Data," NBC News Universal, 2021, https://www.nbcnews.com/politics/politics-news/ufo-report-government-can-t-explain-143-144-mysterious-flying-n1272390.

the U.S. military, and to their dismay, the results contradicted their expectations and suggested extraterrestrials as the catalyst for a significant percentage of the examined reports. This was succeeded in 1949 by the interestingly named *Project Grudge*, resulting in a 600-page report revealing that nearly a fourth of the UFO sightings investigated were unexplainable.[5] And then, there was 2021.

According to the 2021 Unidentified Aerial Phenomenon (UAP) report published by the Office of the Director of National Intelligence (ODNI),[6] there were eighteen incidents reported in which the U.S. military witnessed and documented "unusual movement patterns or flight characteristics," including propulsion or other technology that wasn't evident. Eleven of the incidents were even classified as near misses. The report also made use of the term UAP to describe encounters they were unable to explain.

UAP sounds more formal and scientific than "other" or "UFO," but to their credit, the report said that "the others remain unexplained."[7] This report, which was a

5 Major Boggs, "Project Grudge: Secrets Declassified," 1949, https://www.secretsdeclassified.af.mil/Portals/67/documents/AFD-110719-005.pdf?ver=2016-07-19-142520-690.

6 Mystery Wire, "UFO Report: Government Unable to Explain Aerial Phenomena in Long-Awaited Document," CBS42:Nexstar Media Inc., 2021. https://www.cbs42.com/news/u-s-world/ufo-report-published-by-the-office-of-the-director-of-national-intelligence/.

7 Ibid.

provision of the $2.3 trillion relief bill (i.e., Consolidated Appropriations Act H.R. 133), did not mention aliens as the explanation for the UAPs but did report that the UAPs were cause for concern regarding safety and particularly security in military operations, not to mention national security.[8] As to be expected, portions of the report remained classified, and it can be argued that this is being used for justifying a "slush fund" for more capital. Regardless, the point is that whereas in the past, the U.S. Government went to great lengths to deny, debunk, and even cover up "unexplained aerial phenomenon" (UAP aka UFOs) that they couldn't explain, they've now gone on record to acknowledge and even release footage of what the public refers to as UFOs. So, there's been a tipping point that demonstrates that the belief in extraterrestrial life has become more culturally and academically palatable.

This "new normal" of cultural acceptance is not limited to the United States. Former Israeli Space Security Chief, Haim Eshed, bluntly went on record to state that aliens exist, but humanity simply isn't ready for them. In an interview conducted by Aaron Reich for the *Jerusalem Post* published on December 8, 2020, Eshed stated that there's a "Galactic Federation" which has been in touch with both the U.S. and Israel for years

---

8 Ibid.

but is "keeping to themselves until the time is right."[9] Yes, the former Israeli Space Security Chief publicly said that there's a "Galactic Federation" in an interview he knew would be widely circulated.

One thing has become extremely obvious: UFOs have gone not only mainstream but also international, capturing the attention of governments, intelligence agencies, and militaries around the world. After decades of denial, cover-ups, and even shaming those who made UFO reports, there's now a general acceptance of UFOs and the probability of ETI, which can only mean that there's more disclosure and acceptance to come.

This worldview, the existence of intelligent extraterrestrial life, has been snowballing in its acceptance for a while, and a vast array of people from all walks of life have made this premise fashionable. As recent as the 1960s, UFOs as a topic was generally relegated to coverage by tabloids and science fiction, but not anymore. Dr. Carl Sagan, a well-known 20th-century scientist who, among other things, assisted with the *Voyager 1* project (which included a gold-plated audio-visual disc for communicating with extraterrestrial life forms should it be found by one), said, "I believe the search for extraterrestrial intelligence to be an exceedingly impor-

9 Aaron Reich, "Former Israeli Space Security Chief Says Aliens Exist, Humanity Not Ready," The Jerusalem Post, 2020, https://www.jpost.com/omg/former-israeli-space-security-chief-says-aliens-exist-humanity-not-ready-651405.

tant one for both science and for society."[10] Dr. Chuck Steidel of Cal Tec said, "I would say that the chances of life being out there are very high."[11] Dr. Robert Jastrow, founder of NASA's Goddard Institute and director of the Mount Wilson Observatory, said, "Mankind is on the threshold of entering a large cosmic community."[12] Dr. Kenneth Nealson, who once chaired the National Academy of Sciences Subcommittee for Solar System Exploration, said, "The search for life is no longer a fringe type of thing."[13] Dr. Paul Horowitz, a previous director for BETA (Billion Channel Extraterrestrial Assay), said, "Intelligent life in the universe? Guaranteed. Intelligent life in our galaxy? So overwhelmingly likely that I'd give you almost any odds you'd like."[14]

The U.S. Government and NASA

As the saying goes, "money talks," and the truth is, the U.S. Government has been interested and invested in making contact with ETI since at least *Project Blue Book* and has demonstrated this over the decades by the

10 Sagan and Page, 1996.

11 Fred Heeren, *Show Me God: What the Message from Space Is Telling Us about God* (Wheeling, IL: DayStar Publications, 2000), 37.

12 Ibid.

13 Jim Willson, "Alien World: Startling Discoveries by NASA Scientists Suggest the Universe May Be Teeming with Exotic Life-Forms," *Popular Mechanics*, 1999, 176 (7): 66.

14 Leon Jaroff, "Listening for Aliens," *Time USA, LLC.* (February 5, 1996), 55.

amount of capital they've put into this effort. In 1960, radio astronomer Dr. Frank Drake, then at the National Radio Astronomy Observatory (NRAO), directed a federally funded attempt to detect interstellar radio transmissions based upon the Drake Equation. The Drake Equation is a probability formula presented by Dr. Frank Drake for predicting the odds of intelligent life existing within the Milky Way Galaxy that could also communicate. "The receiver on the 85-foot antenna was tuned to the frequency of the 21-centimeter emission line of interstellar hydrogen. The assumption was that this frequency, 1420 MHz, would be known by any technologically sophisticated society and would constitute a universal hailing frequency."[15]

In 1992, the U.S. Government authorized funding for NASA to search for radio signals generated by extraterrestrial civilizations.[16] There was enough belief in the possibility of ETI (extraterrestrial intelligent life) to constitute a 100-million-dollar investment in the construction of a radio telescope in Puerto Rico, where some of the best scientists would monitor control panels in search of radio waves from ETCs (extra-terrestrial civilizations). Inaudibly, the U.S. Government had an-

---

15 Seth Shostak, "Project Ozma," SETI Institute, 2021, https://www.seti.org/project-ozma.

16 Stephen Garber, "Searching for Good Science: The Cancellation of NASA's SETI Program," *Journal of The British Interplanetary Society*, 52: 3–12, https://history.nasa.gov/garber.pdf.

nounced its belief in the possibility of ETI through its allotment of capital for this and many other related projects.[17] Congress terminated the program in 1993, but it is now operated privately and known as the SETI (Search for Extraterrestrial Intelligence) Institute.[18] Nevertheless, a significant percentage of the capital that NASA spends today is devoted to the hope of discovering extraterrestrial life.

NASA's mission statement says that a component of its purpose is to "...explore the universe and search for life (...) as only NASA can."[19] In 2017, several mainstream media outlets, including the *New York Times*, reported the allocation of $22 million for the AATIP (Advanced Aerospace Threat Identification Program) for a study of UFOs.[20] In 2021, NASA recruited at least twenty-four scholars to participate in a program at Princeton University's Centre of Theological Inquiry (CTI).[21] CTI received a $1.1 million NASA grant in 2014 and sought to learn how the world's major religions would react

---

17 Ibid.

18 Ibid.

19 Andrew C. Revkin, "NASA's Goals Delete Mention of Home Planet," New York Times, 2006, https://www.nytimes.com/2006/07/22/science/22nasa.html.

20 Hannah Sparks, "NASA Hired 24 Theologians to Study Reaction to Aliens: Book," New York Post, 2021, https://nypost.com/2021/12/27/nasa-hired-24-theologians-to-study-reaction-to-aliens-book/.

21 Ibid.

to confirmation of ETI.[22] Dr. Andrew Davidson, who holds a doctorate in biochemistry from Oxford, teaches at Cambridge, and is the author of Astrobiology and Christian Doctrine, is among the participants of the NASA-sponsored program at CTI who believes that the major religions would find it useful to have thought through these implications in advance.[23]

Mainstream Entertainment

Ancient Aliens, a show on the History Channel presented in a documentary-type format, has the goal to present the theory that in ancient times, aliens visited, interacted, and influenced life on earth, a perspective made famous through the 1968 publication of *Chariots of the Gods?* by Erich Von Daniken. Like the book, the show hasn't been without its critics from the more objective wings of archaeology, anthropology, and history asserting that the writers are presenting unverifiable pseudo history. A social media meme of host Giorgio Tsoukalos carries the caption: "I'm not saying it was aliens (...), but it was aliens," poking some good-natured fun at how the show tends to attribute anything unexplainable (to them) as being the work of aliens.[24] Nonetheless, aside

---

22 Ibid.

23 Ibid.

24 "Giorgio Tsoukalos Aliens Memes," Memes Monkey, 2022, https://www.memesmonkey.com/topic/giorgio+tsoukalos+aliens.

from *Pawn Stars*, it has been one of the channel's longest-running and most-watched series within their lineup. Perhaps, more than any other contemporary source, the show has fueled the fires of interest in ETs, and the hosts have rock star like status at UFO conventions. As someone who's traveled to El Fin del Mundo, camped in the Amazon, and hiked in both the Andes and Himalayas, the Travel Channel was a regular on my watch list for the longest time. Once known for its travel programming with hosts like Samantha Brown and the late Anthony Bourdain, as well as shows like *Bizarre Foods, Lonely Planet*, and *Globetrekker*, it was a great resource and inspiration for the typical international traveler. Then in 2016, I noticed there was a shift away from travel towards the paranormal with more of a focus on ghosts, Bigfoot, and UFOs. Why? Ratings, obviously, but also, it's a testament to the fact that the paranormal has become normal.

It wasn't that long ago when words like black magic and witchcraft had somewhat of a medieval ring to our ears, but not any longer. These topics, with UFOs leading the charge, have become a staple for entertainment. UFOs are obviously a topic that people tune in for, and companies are willing to sponsor through advertising. It's as if our culture is being conditioned and programmed for making the paranormal more culturally palatable. After surveying 429 college seniors, the

Skeptical Inquirer (January–February 2006) reported that higher education is now linked to a greater tendency to believe in ghosts and other paranormal phenomenon.[25] Spiritualism, astrology, Bigfoot, ghost hunters, and of course, UFOs have become more acceptable and, dare I say, normal. There has been a paradigm shift.

The Tipping Point Has Tipped in Favor of Accepting UFOs as Real

In 1998 Dr. Peter Sturrock, professor of applied physics at Stanford University, led an independent forum administratively supported by the Society for Scientific Exploration for researching unexplained phenomena. The international panel reviewed the presentations by eight UFO investigators who were asked to present their best cases. They "concluded that some sightings are accompanied by physical evidence that deserves scientific study."[26] In 2020, the U.S. Government pushed the needle a bit further and acknowledged they are in possession of "off-world vehicles not made of this earth."[27]

25 Robert Roy Britt, "Does Education Fuel Paranormal Beliefs?" NBC News Universal, 2006, https://www.nbcnews.com/id/wbna10950526.

26 David F. Salisbury, "Scientific Panel Concludes Some UFO Evidence Worthy of Study," Stanford News Service, 1998, https://news.stanford.edu/pr/98/980629ufostudy.html.

27 Adam K Raymond, "UFO Report: Pentagon Has 'Off-World Vehicles' Not From Earth," New York Intelligencer, 2020, https://nymag.com/intelligencer/2020/07/ufo-report-pentagon-has-off-world-vehicles-not-from-earth.html.

Yes, you read that correctly and may want to read it again: "off-world vehicles not made of this earth." This was also reported on *Tucker Carlson Tonight* on Fox News.[28] Furthermore, The *New York Times* reported that a small group of government officials and scientists believe that objects of "undetermined origin" have crashed to earth and been retrieved.[29] Yes, once again, you read that correctly. Perhaps Americans were still preoccupied with COVID-19 or racial tensions, but for the most part, it seemed as if this announcement was barely newsworthy. And yet, the U.S. Government referenced the existence of "off-world vehicles" and objects of "undetermined origin," inferring that it was what most would decipher and translate as extraterrestrial. Releasing the *Tic-Tac* video[30] and alluding to the access of technology with origins that are "not of this world" further demonstrates that we've crossed a tipping point in our culture's acceptance of UFOs that are simultaneously preparing the world for further disclosure.

---

28 James Rogers and Chris Ciaccia, "With Pentagon UFO Unit in the Spotlight, Report Mentions 'off-World Vehicles Not Made on This Earth,'" Tucker Carlson Tonight: Fox News, 2020, https://www.foxnews.com/science/pentagon-ufo-unit-spotlight-vehicles-earth.

29 Ralph Blumenthal and Leslie Kean, "No Longer in Shadows, Pentagon's U.F.O. Unit Will Make Some Findings Public," New York Times, 2020, https://www.nytimes.com/2020/07/23/us/politics/pentagon-ufo-harry-reid-navy.html.

30 "Watch USS Nimitz 'Tic Tac' UFO: Declassified Video Clip," History Channel: A&E Television Networks, LLC., 2022, https://www.history.com/videos/uss-nimitz-tic-tac-ufo-declassified-video.

A tipping point is when there's enough critical mass to affect mainstream change in cultural and societal norms. In the recent past, it was believed that the fears of chaos and an economic collapse would occur if the U.S. Government disclosed information authenticating ETCs. Introduced in 1950 through the publication of *The Flying Saucers Are Real* by Donald Keyhoe, a former Marine Corp aviator and pulp fiction writer, the "panic theory" for the government's withholding of information was widely circulated, and the ripple effects are still somewhat influential today for rationalizing the withholding of such data.[31] However, with the current trends tipping towards the acceptance of ET life, it wouldn't really be such a shocking idea if most of the general public already accepts this as factual. Are we being conditioned for this?

Compounding surveys from USA Today, Gallup, etc., reveal that approximately two-thirds of Americans believe in the existence of extraterrestrial life within our galaxy.[32] [33] Some will even use the adjective "arrogant" to describe those who don't believe in ETI. Presently, it's still at the front end of the bell curve, but in addition to

31 Donald E. Keyhoe, (Donald Edward), *The Flying Saucers Are Real* (Cosimo Classics, 1950, reprint 2004).

32 Lydia Saad, "Do Americans Believe in UFOs?" Gallup, Inc., 2021, https://news.gallup.com/poll/350096/americans-believe-ufos.aspx.

33 Courtney Kennedy and Arnold Lau, "Most Americans Believe Life on Other Planets Exists," Pew Research Center, 2021, https://www.pewresearch.org/fact-tank/2021/06/30/most-americans-believe-in-intelligent-life-beyond-earth-few-see-ufos-as-a-major-national-security-threat/.

predicting that UFOs will continue to gain mainstream acceptance, we're probably not that far from "E.T. shaming," i.e., you'll be shamed for not believing in aliens. The odds are that you have children, grandchildren, coworkers, and neighbors who believe in extraterrestrial life. In fact, if you don't believe in extraterrestrial life, you're already in the minority. The acceptance of UFOs, ETI, and the paranormal has now tipped towards their existence. More and more people will continue to believe in the existence of intelligent life outside of earth, including the likelihood that earth has and is regularly being visited by aliens.

Clearly, we cannot pretend that the UFO phenomenon is limited to the readers of supermarket tabloids or those who watch more YouTube videos than they should. Rather, it's a worldview that has very clearly infiltrated and permeated nearly every facet of Western civilization, including the Church. Furthermore, in a reflection of postmodern times, the viewer is often left to draw his or her own conclusion about the phenomenon with subjective rather than objective data.

The first thing you should know about UFOs is that not only will the phenomenon continue to gain acceptance, but it will also be seen as a legitimate and worthy subject of study in a variety of academic, scientific, and religious circles.

CHAPTER 2

UFOs and UAPs Have Become More Emboldened and Agressive

The one who gives an answer before he listens—that is his folly and his shame.

(Proverbs 18:13 NET)

UFO reports have been around for a long time. Sometimes referred to as the "Woodcut by Basel," a 1566 piece of art from Switzerland seems to depict red and black orbs over Switzerland that were reportedly *fighting* with each other before sunrise. Since the mid-20th century, UFOs have not only increased their frequency but seem to enjoy making a show of force.

Los Angeles — 1942

UFO sightings are not limited to rural areas and restricted air space but have also been reported and recorded over major metropolitan areas. Several months after Pearl Harbor, air raid sirens were sounded over Los Angeles in the early morning hours of February 24, 1942, subsequently followed by approximately 1,400 rounds of anti-aircraft artillery being fired at a UFO approaching from the Pacific.[34] The only known photograph of the incident was taken over Culver City, California, and shows searchlights focused upon what seems to be a stationary object receiving fire. However, no known aircraft was downed, and the Japanese denied involvement. Until 1987, the U.S. Department of Defense denied having any record of what would become known as the Los Angeles Air Raid,[35] which continued for approximately three hours. The U.S. Army and Navy offered differing explanations for the commotion surrounding the incident and an editorial in the *Los Angeles Times* asked for an investigation.[36] Perhaps Wendell Willkie,

---

34 Lucas Gred, "The Battle of Los Angeles," California State Library, Accessed April 20, 2022, https://cal170.library.ca.gov/february-24-1942-the-battle-of-los-angeles-2/.

35 Wikipedia Contributors, "Battle of Los Angeles – Wikipedia," Wikipedia, The Free Encyclopedia, 2022, https://en.wikipedia.org/wiki/Battle_of_Los_Angeles.

36 Scott Harrison, "From the Archives: The 1942 Battle of L.A.," Los Angeles Times, 2017, https://www.latimes.com/visuals/framework/la-me-fw-archives-1942-battle-la-20170221-story.html.

the 1940 Republican nominee to run against FDR who'd experienced air raids in England, summarized it best by saying, "You won't have to argue about it—you'll just know"[37] (i.e., if you're in an air raid you'll know it and that wasn't one). Many theories have been put forth to explain the incident, but to date, we don't know with certainty what exactly transpired.

It should be noted that this incident occurred just months after Pearl Harbor, and so perhaps those involved were a bit more jittery than normal. Peter Brookesmith said, "From the military point of view, what happened was either a ghastly bungle (if there were no planes) or a depressing display of the 37th CA Brigade (AA)'s terrible marksmanship."[38]

Washington D.C. — 1952

What can upstage the existence of an invasion by flying saucers? Marilyn Monroe. Had it not been for Monroe, who was featured on the cover of *Life* magazine's April 7, 1952 cover, UFOs would have been the featured cover story. Nevertheless, the incident was included on the cover with the caption, "There Is a Case for Inter-

37 Wikipedia Contributors. 2022. "Battle of Los Angeles," Wikipedia, The Free Encyclopedia, 2022, https://en.wikipedia.org/wiki/Battle_of_Los_Angeles.

38 Peter Brookesmith, *UFO: The Complete Sightings Catalogue* (New York: Cassell & Co, 1995).

planetary Saucers."[39] Prior to the *Phoenix Lights*, one of the more publicized UFO reports within the U.S. took place for two consecutive weekends over the nation's capital, Washington D.C., in July 1952. Edward Nugent, an air traffic controller at what was then Washington National Airport, picked up seven objects on his radar approximately fifteen miles southwest of the nation's capital that were not flying any known scheduled flight paths. A fellow air traffic controller, Harry Barnes, who witnessed the objects on Nugent's radar, said, "We knew immediately that a very strange situation existed. Their movements were completely radical compared to those of ordinary aircraft."[40] A quick inspection revealed that there was no reason to suspect equipment malfunction. Barnes proceeded to contact the control tower, where they were informed by controllers Howard Cocklin and Joe Zacko that they too had unidentified blips on their radar screen.[41] Likewise, they too, had witnessed a bright light hovering in the sky that suddenly withdrew at a great speed.

---

39 Liz Ronk, "Marilyn Monroe: LIFE Magazine Covers, 1952-1962," Life, 2022, https://www.life.com/people/marilyn-monroe-life-magazine-covers-photos/.

40 Peter Carlson "50 Years Ago, Unidentified Flying Objects From Way Beyond the Beltway Seized the Capital's Imagination," The Washington Post, 2002, https://www.washingtonpost.com/archive/lifestyle/2002/07/21/50-years-ago-unidentified-flying-objects-from-way-beyond-the-beltway-seized-the-capitals-imagination/59f74156-51f4-4204-96df-e12be061d3f8/.

41 Ibid.

Shortly afterward, a number of objects began to appear on the radar, with several being reported over the White House. Andrews Air Force base was contacted but did not have anything on their radar scopes. However, Airman William Brady reported seeing an "object which appeared to be like an orange ball of fire (...) it was unlike anything I had ever seen before."[42] A commercial pilot for Capital Airlines also witnessed an object, as did Staff Sgt. Charles Davenport, who said, "(the object) would appear to stand still, then make an abrupt change in direction and altitude. This happened several times."[43]

It would seem that these "objects" were capable of dropping out of the pattern *at will*. These UFOs simultaneously disappeared from the radarscopes of those in the area tracking them. On one occasion, they disappeared shortly before the arrival of two F-94 Starfire fighter jets but then returned upon their departure. Gerald Haines, a CIA historian, even makes a reference to "A massive buildup of sightings over the U.S. in 1952, especially in July," which caused the Truman administration to be alarmed.[44]

42 Jerome Clark, *The UFO Book: Encyclopedia of the Extraterrestrial*, Visible Ink Press, 1998, 654.

43 Dan Gilgoff, "Saucers Full of Secrets," Washington City Paper, 2001, https://washingtoncitypaper.com/article/260860/saucers-full-of-secrets/.

44 Gerald K Haines, "CIA's Role in the Study of UFOs, 1947-90," E-Asia Digital Library: Oregon Digital, 1997, https://oregondigital.org/sets/easia/oregondigital:df72rt54c#page/10/mode/1up/search/truman.

Malmstrom Air Force Base — 1967

The *Incident at Malmstrom* on a Montana Air Force base is one that has become a part of UFO lore and remains one of the more enigmatic examples of how national security can be jeopardized by their presence and abilities. On March 24, 1967, a pulsating oval-shaped red UFO was reported by Air Force personnel to be hovering over a missile launch control center.[45] These particular missiles were equipped with nuclear warheads and installed for engaging in nuclear warfare with the Soviet Union (should the need arise). Thus, not only was this restricted air space, but it also required an above top-secret clearance for those deployed to serve there.

Upon seeing the UFO, Air Force First Lieutenant Robert Salas immediately placed a call to his commander First Lieutenant Fred Meiwald.[46] Interestingly, the ten nuclear warheads began shutting down one at a time, as if someone was pushing an off button one at a time, completely disabling them. It was suggested that they'd fallen prey to some form of unexplained electromagnetic pulse (EMP) or that it was simply a technical difficulty—a technical difficulty for which a UFO seems to have been the catalyst.[47] In a personal interview with

---

45 Robert L Hastings, *UFOs and Nukes: Extraordinary Encounters at Nuclear Weapons Sites*, Author House, 2008, 602.

46 Ibid.

47 Hastings, 2008.

Nick Pope, who once served on the UK's Ministry of Defense, he shared that there had been some speculation that aliens had actually powered off nuclear devices in England.[48]

Rendlesham Forest, England — 1980

The U.S. is not the only nation to have experienced UFOs within restricted airspace. Air Force pilots from Iran, Chile, and France have scrambled to investigate UFOs. In 1980, Peruvian Air Force pilot Oscar Santa Maria was even given clearance to fire upon a UFO.[49] The *Rendlesham Forest Incident* (a.k.a. "Britain's Roswell") has the distinction of having occurred within close proximity of *two* Air Force bases.[50] In December of 1980, witnesses spotted unexplained lights coming from the woods.[51] The incident went on for three days and is considered the most well-known UFO incident in the U.K. Several credible witnesses, including trained U.S. Air Force personnel stationed at a Royal Air Force Base,

---

48 Nick Pope, 2022, (UK's Ministry of Defense), interviewed by the author, February 10, Tucson, Arizona.

49 Galan Vazquez, "Terror in the Air: Mission Shoot Down the UFO," Medium, 2020, https://caballodetroy.medium.com/terror-in-the-air-mission-shoot-down-the-ufo-cfd367b07563.

50 "What Happened at the Rendlesham Forest Incident, Britain's Answer to Roswell?" History Channel: A&E Television Networks, LLC., 2022, https://www.history.co.uk/articles/what-happened-at-the-rendlesham-forest-incident-britain-s-answer-to-roswell.

51 Ibid.

and members of the security police team, affirmed the credibility of the incident. Eyewitnesses claimed to have seen a bright light descending into the Rendlesham Forest, and a glowing metallic triangular object was spotted by security personnel in a highly restricted area. Theories such as beams from a lighthouse to a natural phenomenon have been put forth as explanations, but the incident remains unexplained.[52]

Nick Pope, who's extensively researched the incident, granted me an in-person interview on the topic and made it very clear that, without doubt, U.S. Air Force personnel reported seeing an unidentified metallic-looking object hovering over Rendlesham Forest near the Royal Air Force Base. Pope said, "It's claimed that this sighting may have involved the shutdown of nukes. Due to the Official Secrets Act, I cannot comment as to whether or not nuclear weapons were stored at RAF Bentwaters nor RAF Woodbridge, but I can confirm that claims were made that light beams from the UFO penetrated the weapons storage area and had an effect on some of the ordnance."[53]

Mexico City—1991

In regard to UFO sightings with multiple corroborating witnesses, prior to the *Phoenix Lights*, an event

---

52 Ibid.

53 Pope, 2022.

occurring in Mexico City—the world's second-largest city—was one of the better documented UFO events. On July 11, 1991, many citizens of Mexico City were looking to the sky to observe a solar eclipse, but in addition to the eclipse, they unexpectedly noticed and videotaped what looked to be an unidentified flying metallic craft.[54] Two of the witnesses included Guillermo Arragin, a reporter, and Jaime Maussan, a journalist.[55] Sixty miles away, at approximately the same time, a businessman, Luis Lar, also videotaped a UFO in which a shadow appeared to be showing below the object.[56] Another video filmed by the Breton family in Puebla, Mexico, approximately eighty miles southeast of Mexico City, recorded what seemed to be an odd disturbance of the air behind the object.[57] While there may indeed be one, to date, there has never been a satisfactory explanation provided for what millions of people were seeing and recording.

The Phoenix Lights and Governor Symington — 1997

On March 13, 1997, thousands of people witnessed an event that's now referred to as the *Phoenix Lights*. This particular night was especially well documented be-

54 Frances Romero, "Mexico City - 6 UFO Hot Spots Around the World," Time, 2011, http://content.time.com/time/specials/packages/article/0,28804,2072479_2072478_2072471,00.html.

55 Ibid.

56 "Mexico City UFO," Unsolved Mysteries Wiki, Accessed April 20, 2022, n.d., https://unsolvedmysteries.fandom.com/wiki/Mexico_City_UFO.

57 Ibid.

cause, unlike reports that are unanticipated (resulting in blurred photos with few witnesses in isolated areas), this event had many expectant viewers looking to observe the Halle-Bopp comet and was therefore well documented by hundreds of eye-witnesses, many of whom had cameras and video recorders. When Frances Barwood, who was serving on the Phoenix city council at the time, brought up the issue with her peers, they surprisingly seemed dismissive of the event, reflecting a "there's nothing to see here folks, move along" attitude. The U.S. Air Force would later state that the catalyst was most likely misidentified slow-falling illumination flares discharged by an A-10 Warthog aircraft during a training exercise (sometimes referred to as *Operation Snowbird*) at Barry Goldwater Range in southwestern Arizona. Comparative analyses of the lights and the mountain range did indeed reveal a very high similarity of what's referred to as the "second UFO" and was corroborated as a typical training exercise by Capt. Drew Sullins of the Air National Guard,[58] but not the slow-moving blimp-like UFO with a triangular shape.

The answers for the "black triangle" flying north to south, however, remained unconvincing. One of the largest and most unconventional aerial objects had

---

58 "OPERATION SNOWBIRD and The Phoenix Lights Flare Drop | 20th Anniversary of The Phoenix Lights | Interview with Kenny Young 8-5-1997," The UFO Chronicles, 2017, https://www.theufochronicles. com/2017/03/operation-snowbird-phoenix-lights.html.

just flown over the fifth largest metropolitan city in the U.S., with hundreds of eyewitnesses corroborating the event. Fife Symington, who was Arizona's governor at the time, initially seemed cavalier about the event and even spoofed it when a staffer dressed as an alien appeared on stage for a press conference.[59] Ten years later, however, he would go on record stating that he had personally witnessed the occurrence as well. In an episode of *Larry King Live* (July 13, 2007), Symington, a former Air Force pilot, said,

> I acknowledge I saw a craft. I was in the Sunnyslope area around 8 p.m. (...) I went out to look to the West, where (...) all the news channels were filming the Phoenix Lights. And to my astonishment, this large sort of delta-shaped, wedge-shaped craft moved silently over the valley, over Squaw Peak, dramatically large, very distinctive leading edge with some enormous lights. And it just went down to the Southeast Valley. And I was absolutely stunned because I was turning to the west looking for the distant Phoenix Lights, and all of a sudden, this apparition appears.[60]

---

59 "Former Ariz. Governor Boosts UFO Claims," NBC News Universal, 2007, https://www.nbcnews.com/id/wbna17761943.

60 "CNN.Com - Transcripts." 2007. CNN Larry King Live. 2007. https://transcripts.cnn.com/show/lkl/date/2007-07-13/segment/02.

Chicago O'Hare — 2006

There are certain locations like *Area 51* and *Roswell* that have become synonymous with UFOs—Chicago, not so much. On November 7, 2006, a UFO depicted as a dark gray "flying saucer-like object" was reported to be hovering, described by some as silently spinning like a frisbee, over Concourse C, a United Airlines terminal at Chicago O'Hare International airport by airline employees, pilots, and mechanics.[61] The UFO was observed for approximately five minutes and then rapidly departed, moving in a vertical direction, leaving what some described as a "hole in the clouds" above. Prior to the *Chicago Tribune*'s article on the incident, which included material acquired from the Freedom of Information Act, both the Federal Aviation Administration (FAA) and United Airlines denied the event ever took place. In a follow-up report by the National Aviation Reporting Center on Anomalous Phenomena (NARCAP) it was stated that an incident of this nature at a busy airport like O'Hare "constitutes a potential threat to flight safety."[62]

61 Ryan Smith, "O'Hare UFO Sighting in 2006 One of the Most Famous Reported," Chicago Tribune, 2013, https://www.chicagotribune.com/redeye/ct-redeye-xpm-2013-03-20-37880251-story.html.

62 Richard, K. Haines, Efishoff, D. Ledger, L. Lemke, S. Maranto, W. Puckett, T. Roe, M. Shough, and R. Uriarte, "Report by the National Aviation Reporting Center on Anomalous Phenomena (NARCAP) It Was Stated That an Incident of This Nature at a Busy Airport like O'Hare 'Constitutes a Potential Threat to Flight Safety,'" https://static1.squarespace.com/static/5cf80ff422b5a90001351e31/t/5d02ec731230e20001528e2c/1560472703346/NARCAP_TR-10.pdf.

Hangzhou Xiaoshan International Airport, China — 2010

Five of the twenty largest metropolitan cities in the world are in China, and most are never heard of, much less pronounced. Due to a UFO in the area, on July 7, 2010, a commercial airliner going through the typical procedures for landing was denied permission to land.[63] Beginning at approximately 8:40 p.m., approximately eighteen planes were rerouted due to a UFO described as a hovering light emitting red and white rays of light.[64] Some Chinese observers speculated that the object was of U.S. or even Russian origin. However, uploaded photos by local residents suggested more extraterrestrial origins. The incident was of such a pervasive nature that it was inescapable from a government that's generally successful in maintaining a tight lid on any news they do not wish disclosed.

The U.S. Navy 2004–2021

In 2019, the U.S. Navy confirmed that three UFO videos of what they classified as *Unidentified Aerial Phenomena* (UAP aka UFOs) taken by pilots serving on the USS Roosevelt and Nimitz in 2004 were authentic, which pre-

---

63 Mary Huang, "UFO in China's Skies Prompts Investigation," ABC News, 2010, https://abcnews.go.com/International/ufo-china-closes-air-port-prompts-investigation/story?id=11159531.

64 Ibid.

sumes they were not computer-generated nor hoaxed.[65] The three video clips dubbed "FLIR1," "Gimbal," and "Go Fast" are video records of aerial encounters between U.S. Navy aircraft and what they classified as UAPs.[66] In all three videos, the UFOs performed maneuvers that cannot be executed using current known aviation technology. David Fravor, a sixteen-year veteran and participant in the Navy's famed "Top Gun" program, who flew one of the F-18 Hornet fighters in the *Gimbal* video, described it as resembling a flying "Tic Tac" (breath mint) that was approximately 25-feet long, with no markings, wings, no exhaust, nor discernible propulsion.[67] He also reported that it rapidly ascended to 12,000 feet and finally accelerated away at a speed that he suggested was "well above supersonic."[68] The pilot of the other F-18 Hornet, Alex Dietrich, one of the Navy's first female fighter pilots, said, "Yeah, so we were launched and expecting to do this routine training mission off the coast of Southern California when we were vectored to intercept a real-world contact that the USS Princeton, one of the other ships in our battle group, was picking up on their radar. And when we merged with it, we

---

65 Jacquelyn Kinick, "Navy Pilots Recall 'Unsettling' 2004 UAP Sighting," 60 Minutes - CBS News, 2021, https://www.cbsnews.com/news/navy-ufo-sighting-60-minutes-2021-05-16/.

66 Ibid.

67 Ibid.

68 Ibid.

saw something weird in the water, some disturbance, and then we saw this weird flying Tic Tac shaped object that we engaged with, and it disappeared almost as fast and abruptly as it came into the picture. And we were shocked, we were confused, we were alarmed that we couldn't identify it visually."[69]

The Navy apparently never intended for the videos to be made public, but due to a series of loopholes within the Freedom of Information Act (FOIA), the TTSA's (To the Stars Academy of Arts and Science) request for accessing them was surprisingly granted, and the story was reported by the *Washington Post* in 2017. The Pentagon confirmed that the videos were authentic, but they did not have an explanation nor answer for what exactly they were.[70] For unknown craft to be able to freely operate within the vicinity of what would be considered restricted military air space and during military maneuvers should be cause for concern for all of us. This, however, is not the first time UFOs have invaded restricted airspace, nor will it be the last.

Reading between the lines, it appears that the aggressive posturing of UFOs has prompted more research and development for defense should they become hos-

69 Jeremy Corr, "Lt. Cmdr. Alex Dietrich," GoodStory, 2021, https://good-story.io/lt-cmdr-alex-dietrich/.

70 Kayla Epstein, "Navy Admits UFO Videos Are Real, but Would like to Stop Using 'UFO' - The Washington Post," The Washington Post, 2019, https://www.washingtonpost.com/national-security/2019/09/18/those-ufo-videos-are-real-navy-says-please-stop-saying-ufo/.

tile. In 2017, perhaps earlier, the U.S. Department of Defense (DoD) initiated the Unexplained Aerial Phenomenon Task Force, assigned with the investigation of UFO encounters at military installations. In June 2021, a much-anticipated disclosure reported that since 2004, one-hundred forty-four UFO sightings had been investigated and filed under categories such as "airborne clutter," "natural atmospheric phenomenon," "output from government or industrial programs," and "foreign adversary systems."[71]

The most popular category, "other" (aka UFOs), requires additional scientific advances for interpreting their nature. A nine-page public report from the Office of the Director of National Intelligence (ODNI) concluded that since they were able to be detected by radar, these objects were most likely tangible.[72] However, the report also said, "UAP clearly posed a safety of flight issue and may pose a challenge to U.S. national security.[73] Safety concerns primarily center on aviators contending with an increasingly cluttered air domain. UAP would also represent a national security challenge if they are foreign adversary collection platforms or provide evidence a potential adversary has developed

---

71 The Office of the Director of National Intelligence, "Preliminary Assessment: Unidentified Aerial Phenomena," 2021, no. June: 1–9.

72 Ibid, 3.

73 Ibid, 3.

either a breakthrough or disruptive technology."[74] In November 2021, the Pentagon revealed the formation of the Airborne Object Identification and Management Synchronization Group to oversee UFO investigations (sounds a bit like X-Files, doesn't it?). Then on December 15, 2021, the U.S. Senate approved a $770 billion defense bill that included (under section 1683) the creation of an agency for the purpose of investigating UFOs (aka UAP).[75] The Pentagon obviously doesn't see the UFO phenomenon going away anytime soon.

People Are Seeing Something

Not only have journalists, reporters, and the general public made UFO reports, but so have a vast array of elected officials, astronauts, and aviation engineers who've gone on record to report their encounters, including presidents.

U.S. Presidents

Although President Carter clarified in a 2005 GQ magazine interview entitled "The Gospel According to Jimmy" by Will Hylton that his usage of "unidentified" didn't necessitate that it was extraterrestrial, in 1973, he said, "I don't laugh at people anymore when people say

---

74 Ibid, 3.

75 Samuel Chamberlain and Bruce Golding, "$770B Defense Bill Includes Agency to Investigate UFOs," New York Post, 2021, https://nypost.com/2021/12/15/770b-defense-bill-includes-agency-to-investigate-ufos/.

they've seen a UFO because I've seen one myself."[76] His predecessor, President Gerald Ford, said, "I think there may be something of substance to these (UFO) reports (...) In the firm belief that the American public deserves a better explanation than that thus far given by the Air Force, I strongly recommend that there be a committee investigation of the UFO phenomena. I think we owe it to the people to establish credibility regarding UFOs and to produce the greatest possible enlightenment of the subject."[77] A second-hand report claims that in 1974, Ronald Reagan, who was then governor of California, along with three others aboard a Cessna Citation, had a UFO encounter. As the airplane approached Bakersfield, California, the passengers called the pilot's attention to a strange object to their rear.

"It appeared to be several hundred yards away," pilot Bill Paynter recalled. "It was a fairly steady light until it began to accelerate. Then it appeared to elongate. Then the light

76 Thomas O'Toole, "UFO Over Georgia? Jimmy Logged One," The Washington Post, 1977, https://www.washingtonpost.com/archive/politics/1977/04/30/ufo-over-georgia-jimmy-logged-one/080ef1c3-6ff3-41a9-a1e4-a37c54b5cbca/.

77 Frank Warren, "Ford's UFO Legacy: Unapproving of The Air Force's Explanation He Requests Congressional Investigation," The UFO Chronicles, 2006, https://www.theufochronicles.com/2006/12/fords-ufo-legacy-unapproving-of-air.html.

took off. It went up at a 45-degree angle at a high rate of speed."[78]

A week later, Reagan recounted the sighting to Norman C. Miller, then Washington bureau chief for the *Wall Street Journal*. Reagan told Miller, "We followed it for several minutes. It was a bright white light. We followed it to Bakersfield, and all of a sudden to our utter amazement it went straight up into the heavens."[79] When Miller expressed some doubt, a "look of horror came over [Reagan]. It suddenly dawned on him that he was talking to a reporter."[80] Immediately afterward, according to Miller, Reagan "clammed up." Reagan did not discuss the event again, at least not publicly.[81] There is an anecdotal account of Reagan discussing the sighting at a private party in Lucille Ball's memoir, in which Ball reportedly said, "After he was elected president, I kept thinking about that event, and wondered if he still would have won if he told everyone he had seen a flying saucer."[82]

78 John B Alexander, UFOs: Myths, Conspiracies, and Realities, Thomas Dunne Books, 2011, https://www.amazon.com/UFOs-Conspiracies-John-Alexander-Ph-D/dp/125000201X.

79 The Editors of Publications International, Ltd., "Ronald Reagan Sees a UFO." How Stuff Works, 2022, https://science.howstuffworks.com/space/aliens-ufos/ronald-reagan-ufo.htm.

80 Ibid.

81 Ibid.

82 Jim Brochu, *Lucy in the Afternoon: An Intimate Memoir of Lucille Ball* (New York: William Morrow & Co., 1990).

International Diplomats

Paul Hellyer, a Canadian Minister of Defense from 1963 to 1967, as well as Haim Eshed, a former Israeli Space Security Chief, have both gone on public record expressing their belief in the existence of ETI.[83] Kirsan Ilyumzhinov, the "president" of Kalmykia, an "autonomous" republic of the Russian Federation, reported that he was abducted by aliens in yellow suits from his Moscow apartment in 1997 who communicated with him by telepathy.[84] The Russians were not that skeptical about his encounter but at least one member of their parliament was concerned if he'd disclosed any classified information. *The Atlantic* reported that Andrei Lebedev, a member of Russia's parliament, sent a formal letter to Dmitry Medvedev, demanding that Ilyumzhinov submit to an interrogation.[85]

---

83 Kashmira Gander, "Former Canadian Defense Secretary Paul Hellyer Calls on Governments to Reveal UFO Information," The Independent, 2015, https://www.independent.co.uk/news/world/americas/former-canadi

84 Paul Goldman and Adela Suliman, "Former Israeli Space Security Chief Says Extraterrestrials Exist, and Trump Knows about It," NBC News Universal, 2020, https://www.nbcnews.com/news/weird-news/former-israeli-space-security-chief-says-extraterrestrials-exist-trump-knows-n1250333.

85 Alex Eichler, "Russian Head of State Claims Space-Alien Contact," The Atlantic, 2010, https://www.theatlantic.com/international/archive/2010/05/russian-head-of-state-claims-space-alien-contact/340920/.

Clarence "Kelly" Johnson (Aeronautical and Systems Engineer, "Skunk Works")

Beginning with the twin-engine design of the distinct P-38 Lightning in 1938, Johnson contributed to the design of over thirty aircraft. He is best known and credited with designing Lockheed's U-2 spy plane and SR-71 Blackbird. Johnson served as an integral part of Skunk Works, the pseudonym for Lockheed Martin's Advanced Developmental Programs. A career aeronautical engineer, his list of accomplishments is without comparison and for most of his life, he was on the cutting edge of aviation. However, in 1953 he made a UFO report that he described as looking like a "saucer" that suddenly gained elevation and departed at such a speed that he considered it to be beyond earthly aeronautics. "Unknown to Johnson, a Lockheed flight test crew, which included the company's chief aerodynamics engineer, chief flight test engineer, and two highly experienced test pilots, observed the same object while flying northwest along the Los Angeles coastline. Unsurprisingly, Johnson and the flight crew's descriptions of the incident are meticulously detailed. Most importantly, Lockheed's engineers and pilots explicitly ruled out a cloud formation as a plausible explanation for the incident."[86] Johnson said, "I have definitely believed in

86 Marik von Rennenkampff, "UFOs, the Channel Islands and the Navy's 'Drone Swarm' Mystery," MSN: The Hill, 2022, https://thehill.com/opinion/national-security/588223-ufos-the-channel-islands-and-the-navys-drone-swarm-mystery/.

the possibility that flying saucers exist—this in spite of a good deal of kidding from my technical associates. Having seen this particular object on December 16th, I am now more firmly convinced than ever that such devices exist, and I have some highly technical converts in this belief as of that date."[87]

Astronaut Gordon Cooper

"I believe that these extraterrestrial vehicles and their crews are visiting this planet from other planets and are obviously more advanced than we are here on earth (...) Also, I did have occasion in 1959 to have two days of observation of many flights of them (UFOs), of different sizes, flying in higher formation, generally from east to west over Europe,"[88] said Cooper. He also said, "I believe that these extraterrestrial vehicles and their crews are visiting the planet from other planets that are a little more technically advanced than we are on earth."[89]

---

87 Ibid.

88 Dave Wheeler, "Astronaut Gordon Cooper Talks About UFO Sightings," 96.1 The Eagle, Townsquare Media, Inc., 2012, https://961theeagle.com/astronaut-gordon-cooper-talks-about-ufo-sightings/.

89 Timothy Good, Above Top Secret. New York: William Morrow Co., https://www.amazon.com/Above-Secret-Timothy-Good-1988-06-03/dp/B01FIYTAJ4/ref=tmm_hrd_swatch_0?_encoding=UTF8&qid=&sr=.

Pilots and Air Traffic Controllers

UFOs have been witnessed by military pilots and tracked by the best of radar equipment and air traffic controllers who have reported seeing them performing maneuvers that defy our current understanding of physics and aeronautics. One of the more notable, taking place in the Desert Southwest occurred on March 21, 1995, when an America West airline flight en route to Las Vegas was over New Mexico. The crew reported a UFO to the Air Traffic Control Center in Albuquerque. When lightning flashed behind the object, it was reported as being a large cigar-shaped object guesstimated as 300 to 500 feet in length. The following is an excerpt from the transcript of their dialogue:

America West 564: Cactus 564 ... off to our 3:00, got some strobes out there. Could you tell us what it is?

Albuquerque Air Traffic Control: Uh, Uh ... I'll tell you what, that's some, uh ... right now ... I don't know what it is right now. That is restricted area that is used by the military out there during the day.

AW-564: Yeah ... it's pretty odd.

ABQ: Hold on ... let me see if anybody else knows around here.

AW-564: Cactus 564, can you paint the object at all on your radar?

ABQ: Cactus 564 ... No, I don't, and in talking to three or four guys around here no one knows what that is, never heard about that.

AW-564: Cactus 564 ... nobody's painting it at all?

ABQ: Cactus 564 say again?

AW-564: I said there's nothing on their radars on the other centers at all on that (garbled) clear area ... that object that's up in the air?

ABQ: Uh? It's up in the air?

AW-564: Affirmative!

ABQ: No. No one knows anything about it. What's the altitude about?

AW-564: I don't know, right around 30,000 or so. And it's uh ... there's a strobe that starts ... um, going on counterclockwise, and uh ... the length is unbelievable.[90]

Christian Encounters

In case you're wondering, even evangelical Christians are among those who have made UFO reports. A friend of mine, Pastor Paul Fredericks, who's been in ministry for decades, was also a witness to the *Phoenix*

---

90 John Greenewald, "America West Airlines Flight 564 UFO Case - May 25, 1995," The Black Vault Case Files, 2021, https://www.theblackvault.com/casefiles/america-west-airlines-flight-564-ufo-case/.

Lights. For a brief season, we were in the same Sunday School class for newlyweds. In his words:

> I was traveling north and at the intersection of Scottsdale and Bell Roads when I saw the lights that were moving exceptionally slow. There were a few cars pulled over, and others were also viewing it, but in my mind, I instantly processed it as being an Air Force experiment. Before going into ministry, I was employed by an aircraft parts manufacturer in Cleveland, and whereas we didn't use the terminology of stealth to describe it in the 1980s, we'd heard that the government was working on an "invisible airplane" and so that's what I presumed it was.[91]

Although my father wasn't a born-again Christian at the time, my first discussion about the topic of UFOs was with my parents. My father served in the U.S. Navy for twenty years, and towards the end of his career, he would commute from Roanoke, Virginia to Norfolk, Virginia, where he was stationed. It was about a four-hour drive along Route 460. I remember him coming home one time, and as usual, I'd run in to see him. However,

---

91 Paul Fredricks (Pastor), Interview on the *Phoenix Lights* with the author, January 29, 2022.

I noticed that he was in a very deep conversation with my mother and had a very disturbed look on his face. I was approximately nine years old, and seeing that I was unsettled by my father's disposition, my mother, a born-again Christian, said, "Son, your dad saw a flying saucer."

At this time, my childhood friends and I were obsessed with building Aurora monster models (Godzilla, The Creature from the Black Lagoon, etc.), and we lived our lives around a tv show entitled *Kolchak: The Night Stalker* starring Darrin McGavin, about a Chicago reporter who had regular run-ins with vampires, monsters, etc. Thus, I was excited to get more information from my father, but it was very obvious it was something he didn't care to discuss.

Nevertheless, it was a moment etched in my mind, and while we were having coffee one morning in 2021, I brought up the topic and asked if he remembered the incident. He did. He recalled that while traveling one night just east of Appomattox, Virginia, on Route 460, he saw an unusual object with many lights, which he described as looking something like a "flying tractor-trailer." For fear of ridicule, he never discussed it with anyone but my mother and me, but weeks later, other reports surfaced in the newspaper, giving him a sense of relief that he had not been the only one to see it. I still remember him showing us a newspaper article reporting this.

After having an article published on the subject of UFOs in the *Christian Research Journal*,[92] a magazine whose readership is predominantly comprised of Christians who enjoy studying theology and apologetics, I received several letters from readers who wanted to impress upon me that "UFOs are real!" The following is an example of one letter that I received:

> In the spring of 1961, a colleague and I were aboard a plane returning from a meeting in Huntsville, where we had gone to discuss with space officials the future role of semiconductors in space exploration. The flight from Huntsville to Pittsburgh had been uneventful. We were cruising about 18–20,000 feet at about 500 mph. Sitting near the window on the left side of the plane, I was peering at a black night when I suddenly saw a light "thing" that was obviously tracking the flight of our plane but at the same time, was performing an elevator-like sweep of the sky while tracking the flight of our plane. After a few moments, I asked my engineering colleague to look out the window and tell me

92 Bobby Brewer, "Seven Things You Should Know about UFOs," Christian Research Institute, 2002, 25 (2), http://web.archive.org/web/20210520005553/https://www.equip.org/article/seven-things-you-should-know-about-ufos/.

what he saw. Without further discussion, he described to me what I had seen. Neither of us had any kind of idea of what was taking place. Shortly, the plane's co-pilot came out of the cockpit with a searchlight in his hand. He played the searchlight out of our window onto the plane's left-wing motor. I asked him what he was trying to do. He explained that the cockpit instruments displayed a loss of oil pressure in the plane's left engine. Finding nothing obvious from his searchlight effort, he returned to the cockpit. My colleague and I watched the "thing" tracking our plane, still behaving like an elevator making sharp "straight up and down" sweeps while keeping abreast of the plane's horizontal level of flight. This continued for several minutes—perhaps eight to ten minutes. To some degree, we were "scared to death."

After this period of several minutes had passed, my colleague and I were glued to watching this strange behavior—the "thing" took off in level flight at a speed several times the speed of our plane—something estimated at more than Mach 3 or Mach 4. The "thing" simply disappeared in the night.[93]

---

93 Anonymous Letter to the Author, May 19, 2002.

For over half a century, astronauts, cosmonauts, pilots, police officers, and airline and airport personnel have been reporting UFOs and UAPs. Leslie Keane, an investigative reporter who has boldly delved into this specific aspect of UFOs and has dedicated an entire book to the subject appropriately entitled *UFOs: Generals, Pilots, and Government Officials Go on the Record*, in which she documents the eyewitness testimonies of UFO encounters from Tehran, Iran to Chicago's O'Hare airport. Her contributors are an impressive list of military pilots as well as those who spent the better part of their lives within the FAA or air traffic control. In her concluding thoughts, she says, "This book has accomplished, in my view, the presentation of some of the most compelling evidence—only a slice of it; we must remember that UFOs *do exist*. We have seen that there are solid, three-dimensional objects of unknown origin flying in our skies."[94]

IFOs (Identified Flying Objects)

Although there's no doubt that people are seeing and experiencing unexplainable phenomena, before moving forward, it's important to note that regardless of the credentials of an eyewitness, the fact that something is unidentifiable should not instantaneously necessitate

---

94 Leslie Kean, UFOs: Generals, Pilots, and Government Officials Go on the Record, (New York: Rivers Press, 2010), 291.

a conclusion of extraterrestrial origins, i.e., UFO does not necessitate ETI. "Mark the word unidentified and note that it is the term that the individual making the report ascribes to the flying object," and "simply means that it is unidentifiable to the observer."[95] For example, from 1947 to 1969, the U.S. Air Force investigated UFOs under the name *Project Blue Book*, and a significant percentage of the 12,618 UFO cases investigated had exceptionally questionable and even ridiculous explanations (e.g., swamp gas); some did indeed have plausible explanations.[96]

On April 16, 2021, the Toronto Sun published an article with a heading that declared, "Video of UFOs taken by U.S. warship called 'best world has ever seen.'"[97] The now famous (at least in UFO circles) video, reportedly filmed by sailors aboard the USS Russell, shows triangular or pyramid-shaped UFOs that were filmed in 2019. The Pentagon confirmed the film's authenticity, but initially, they didn't clarify exactly what that meant. It wasn't until later that Pentagon spokesman Susan

95 Robert Brewer, *UFOs: 7 Things You Should Know*, Publish America, 2006, 25.

96 "Project BLUE BOOK - Unidentified Flying Objects," National Archives: Military Records, 2020, https://www.archives.gov/research/military/air-force/ufos?_ga=2.168296481.1048005295.1651673900-559772480.1651673900#usafac.

97 *Toronto Sun*, "Video of UFO taken by U.S. warship called best 'world has ever seen," April 16, 2021, https://torontosun.com/news/weird/video-of-ufos-taken-by-u-s-warship-called-best-world-has-ever-seen.

Gough said, "I can confirm that the referenced photos and videos were taken by Navy personnel."[98] However, Mick West, who is an expert at debunking conspiracy theories by applying objective reasoning, said that in regards to the pyramid video, upon further review, "The simplest explanation is that it's just a plane."[99] *The Proof is Out There*, a television show on the History Channel hosted by veteran journalist Tony Harris, who, unlike most shows of this genre, is not afraid to call a hoax a hoax, also concluded that due to the fact that the lights are flashing at the exact same frequency that is expected of aircraft, the "pyramid video" is most likely an airplane.

UFOs Are Always One Step Ahead

Furthermore, before proceeding, it is also noteworthy that many UFO sightings are only about one generation ahead of known aeronautics. Interestingly, there are no known documented pre-1965 reports of anyone being beamed aboard a spacecraft, a la *Star Trek*—*Star Trek* debuted in 1966. Furthermore, before Apollo 11, aliens often claimed to be from the moon or Venus,

---

98 Eleanor Watson, "Pentagon Confirms Authenticity of Videos Showing Unidentified Flying Objects., CBS News, 2021, https://www.cbsnews.com/news/ufo-video-authenticity-pentagon/.

99 Steven Greenstreet and Jackie Salo, "UFO Expert Debunks Navy Footage of Pyramid-Shaped Objects," New York Post, 2021, https://nypost.com/2021/04/21/ufo-expert-debunks-navy-footage-of-pyramid-shaped-objects/.

but not anymore. Since July 20, 1969, aliens claim to be from locations so distant that, at this time, it would be impossible to verify, and we're left with taking them at their word regarding their origin.

Why do they keep changing their story? As technology has progressed, so have the appearance, origin, and capabilities of aliens. It is my opinion (and prediction) that in the near future, UFO phenomena will move away from crafts being occupied by extraterrestrial beings toward drones, hybrids, and artificial intelligence (AI) from ETCs.

UFOs seem to change with the times. For example, some of the UFO reports from the late 1800s were described as "airships" or "flying cigars," which are remarkably similar to zeppelins and blimps. By today's standards, the idea of traversing galaxies in hot air balloons or blimps is implausible. On November 17, 1896, hundreds of Californians reported seeing a large "electric arc lamp" over Sacramento.[100] Three years later, a report was made in France of a round luminous object that rose above the horizon and then shrunk in size as it moved into the distance.[101] Ten years later, an artist's sketch of a UFO report in Peterborough, England, looked strikingly similar to a blimp.[102] A very similar

---

100 Brookesmith, 1995, 23.

101 Ibid, 23.

102 Ibid, 26.

object was reported over Manhattan Island, New York, in 1910. Hundreds of Manhattan residents reported seeing a bulky object circle the Metropolitan building, which then flew toward the Flatiron Building before it returned to the Madison Square area.[103]

Battlefield blimps first appeared in 1794, and even today, they're a facet of the Army's arsenal. In August 2009, it was reported that blimps were being reconsidered for use by the U.S. Army.[104] Able to detect cruise missiles from up the 300 miles away, *Popular Science* published an article stating that a $1.4-billion blimp "carries radar that can see 360 degrees and track down terrain-hugging cruise missiles up to 300 miles away. Another planned blimp would carry fire-control radar to provide targeting info, helping surface-to-air missile systems intercept and shoot down incoming threats, which may also include large rockets and ballistic missiles in the early ascent phase."[105] It's still a mystery, but some of the descriptions of the altitude and movement of the "black boomerang" from the *Phoenix Lights* incident had very "blimp-like" qualities. Therefore, we must

---

103 Ibid, 27.

104 Jeremy Hsu, "Battlefield Blimp Tracks Low-Flying Cruise Missiles," 2009, Popular Science, 2009. https://www.popsci.com/military-aviation-amp-space/article/2009-08/battlefield-blimp-tracks-ground-hugging-cruise-missiles/.

105 Ibid.

also take into consideration that, in some cases, UFOs are actually EFOs (experimental flying objects).

EFOs — Experimental Flying Objects

U.S. Military research and development must also be considered and possibly explains why so many UFO reports take place within the Desert Southwest and often within the vicinity known as *Area 51*, which is administered by Nellis Air Force Base. Located north of Las Vegas, Nevada, on a dry lake, *Area 51* initially provided the ideal seclusion and conditions for experimental military aircraft such as the U-2, A-12, SR-71, SR-72, F-117, YF-118G, X-45A, etc., some of which could have been described as alien in appearance to the average observer.

The TR-3 (Black Manta) is the name given to a speculative military aircraft that may explain the "black triangle" UFOs that were described as the *Belgian Wave* that occurred from 1989–1992, as well as the *Phoenix Lights* (1997), the *St. Clair* (Illinois) *Triangle* (2000), and the *Tinley Park Lights* (2004–06).[106] Described as an experimental sub-sonic stealth reconnaissance aircraft resembling a flying triangle, the TR-3 may have been patented as early as 1977 by Teledyne Rand, which, if not Tactical Reconnaissance, may explain the "TR" designation as well as many UFO sightings.

---

106 Bill Yenne, *Area 51 – Black Jets: A History of the Aircraft Developed at Groom Lake, America's Secret Aviation Base* (Minneapolis: Zenith Press, 2014).

Aurora (aka SR-91) is the moniker given to an experimental reconnaissance hypersonic aircraft that technically doesn't exist but is thought by some to have been used for experimenting with using pulse wave detonation resulting in sonic booms and unusual contrails resembling knots on a rope or donuts on a string. The "Black Manta" and "Aurora" may be one in the same and are believed by some aviation writers to have been the B-2's prototype and predecessor.

The moniker "Aurora" was ascribed to the alleged craft as the result of a leaked budget report from 1985. It is described as looking like a black triangle which, in addition to employing stealth technology, was being used in the 1990s to experiment with hypersonic aircraft propulsion, and reportedly able to reach an altitude of 135,000 feet, serving as a supplement to spy satellites.[107] [108] In 1993, Bill Sweetman, author of books such as *F-22 Raptor* and *Inside the Stealth Bomber*, suggested that Aurora as a project did indeed exist and that, most likely, technological progress finally "caught up with the ambition that launched the program a generation ago."[109] Eyewitness reports of Aurora all but dis-

107 "Aurora (Spyplane)," Aircraft Wiki, 2022, https://aircraft.fandom.com/wiki/Aurora_(spyplane).

108 Wikipedia Contributors, "Aurora (Aircraft)," Wikipedia, The Free Encyclopedia, 2022, https://en.wikipedia.org/wiki/Aurora_(aircraft).

109 Bill Sweetman, "The Top-Secret Warplanes of Area 51," Popular Science, 2006, https://www.popsci.com/military-aviation-space/article/2006-10/top-secret-warplanes-area-51/.

appeared by 2000, leaving us to wonder if the program was scrapped for something else, or perhaps they had achieved their goal. Imagine seeing an F-117 Nighthawk *before* its maiden flight in 1981. Imagine what's being tested now. For example, an article in Forbes magazine entitled *What Is Behind the U.S. Navy's 'Fusion Energy' Patent?* by Ariel Cohen alludes to technological advancements in avionics as a possible explanation for the "Tic Tac" UFOs.[110]

Although it is not the explanation that a spiritually hungry culture is looking for, and one that many "Close Encounter Wannabes" are quick to dismiss, experimental military aircraft must be taken into account for explaining a significant percentage of the UFO phenomenon. Militaries, not limited to the U.S., regularly develop weapons for national defense purposes in secret, which very well may explain both experimental as well as reconnaissance craft that can look very "alien" from a distance. Rational explanations do not go viral in this postmodern era, but the truth is still the truth, so it must be noted that a percentage of UFO reports have earthly origins and explanations. *Stay with me. We're going to get to some of the more sensational aspects of the phenomenon shortly,* but to ascribe every UFO and unexplained aerial phenomenon to the work of extrater-

---

110 Ariel Cohen, "What Is Behind The U.S. Navy's 'UFO' Fusion Energy Patent?" Forbes, 2021, https://www.forbes.com/sites/arielcohen/2021/02/08/what-is-behind-the-us-navys-ufo-fusion-energy-patent/?sh=31a1ac854733.

restrial activity would simply be sloppy scholarship and lacking in wisdom. There's yet more to consider—the challenge of space travel.

Following the success of NASA's manned missions to the moon (1969–1975), it was presumed that Mars would be next. But the last set of footprints to be left on another "world" was made by astronaut Eugene Ceren of Apollo 17 in 1972.[111] [112] Why? As it turns out, space travel is a bit complicated, risky, and expensive. It is not the purpose of this book to explore the intricacies of space travel's dilemmas: food and water supplies for the crew, fuel, asteroids, space debris, radiation exposure, and time (just to name a few), but if we were able to utilize a spacecraft that could travel at the speed of light it would take over fifty years (yes, years) to reach the next closest star system and that's without a money-back guarantee that you'd even encounter another intelligent civilization there. Although proponents of ETCs are quick to propose that unknown transportation technologies and wormholes (stargates) might exist, enabling ETs to visit earth, it's worth noting that there are some serious dilemmas to consider for space travel for any biological being.

111 "Man's Last Footsteps On The Moon Historical Marker," The Historical Marker Database, 2022, https://www.hmdb.org/m.asp?m=62881.

112 Elizabeth Howell, "Eugene Cernan: Last Man on the Moon," Space, 2017, https://www.space.com/20790-eugene-cernan-astronaut-biography.html.

Although, in theory and on paper, an intergalactic portal—a "wormhole" (aka Einstein-Rosen bridge)—would enable the connection of galactic civilizations billions of light-years apart, technically it's never been demonstrated as viable. Even the brightest minds acknowledge that while theoretically possible, such a portal would be dangerously unstable and unpredictable, not to mention the fatal impact upon humans, and presumably other biological beings, from the resulting g-forces. If, however, there were biological entities traveling in crafts from distant galaxies, extraterrestrials would also have to deal with the hurdles of space travel. This may explain the recent shift in terminology of using UAP in place of UFOs. In 2016 when Jimmy Kimmel asked presidential candidate Hillary Clinton about UFOs, she corrected his terminology by saying, "You know, there's a new name. It's *Unexplained Aerial Phenomenon*. That's the latest nomenclature."[113]

As a result of directing the United Kingdom's UFO investigation program, Nick Pope was sometimes referred to as the British Fox Mulder. In a personal interview, he revealed that not only was UAP his suggestion to make the topic a bit more palatable to government and military representatives but that it also covered a broader spectrum beyond tangible objects. "UAP pro-

113 AJ Vicens, "Hillary Clinton Is Serious About UFOs," Mother Jones, 2016, https://www.motherjones.com/politics/2016/03/hillary-clinton-and-ufo-thing-just-wont-go-away/.

vides a broader range of explanations which are not bound or limited to biological ETs in spacecraft as the only answer for the phenomenon," said Pope.[114] *I predict that with aeronautical and technological advances, the cosmic goalposts will continually change in regard to the ET's origins.*

As a result of this reality, some of the other theories being put forth to accommodate intergalactic travel propose that UFOs and their pilots are actually mechanical probes or advanced hybrid forms of AI: robots. This may explain why, so far, no one has ever reported seeing a restroom, nor breakroom for that matter, aboard an alien spacecraft. On September 25, 2019, NASA announced plans to experiment with testing shape-shifting robots to explore Saturn's moons.[115] Space travel can be bad for the health of any biological being.

As our knowledge of science and technology grows, the answer to who is piloting the UFOs will continually pivot to accommodate any scientific or technological advances. Space travel isn't as easy as it appears in science fiction. Nevertheless...

The second thing you should know about UFOs is that people are seeing and experiencing unexplained aerial phenomena that doesn't reso-

---

114 Pope, 2022.

115 Arielle Samuelson, "NASA Designing Shapeshifting Robots for Saturn's Moons," Webpage of NASA Jet Propulsion Laboratory, 2019, https://www.jpl.nasa.gov/news/nasa-designing-shapeshifting-robots-for-saturns-moons.

nate with our current knowledge of avionics or physics.

This begs the question—Who's piloting the spaceships?

As Ufologist Stanton Friedman once quipped, "never mind the saucers, what about the occupants?"[116] If the pilots are not ET biological entities, alien engineered A.I., or self-replicating drones, then who or what are they? We'll discuss this in an upcoming chapter, but before proceeding, *I predict that earthlings will become more, not less, gullible.*

116 "Full Text of 'David Jacobs The UFO Controversy In America,'" Internet Archive, 2014, https://archive.org/stream/DavidJacobsTheUFOControversyInAmerica/Nick Pope - The Uninvited - An Expose of the Alien Abduction Phenomenon_djvu.txt.

CHAPTER 3

Earthlings are Gullible

History has shown that often there seems to be a vacuum, and then pseudo-science takes over. Once the vacuum has been created, a new prophet emerges. Some members of a gullible public will be waiting to follow the leader, even though it involves the wearing of a mental blindfold.[117]

—Dr. Clifford Wilson

On October 30, 1938, an adaptation of the H.G. Wells Science Fiction classic, *War of the Worlds*, was aired over the CBS (Columbia Broadcasting System) radio airwaves by *The Mercury Theater*, resulting in panic and misleading many listeners to presume the events to be real.[118] The episode was presented in a simulated news-

---

117 Clifford Wilson, *The Chariots Still Crash* (New York, Signet, 1976), 7-8.

118 Troy Brownfield, "War of the Worlds: The Greatest Halloween Prank in American History." The Saturday Evening Post, 2018, https://www.saturdayeveningpost.com/2018/10/war-of-the-worlds-the-greatest-halloween-prank-in-american-history/.

cast-style reporting, portraying the invasion of earth by Martians in what could be described as a radio version of staged reality television, and many Americans bought it hook, line, and sinker—some things never change. This, it should be noted, was in spite of the fact that the episode was introduced as a fictional dramatization including three additional disclaimers interspersed throughout the presentation.

On the following day, *The Watertown* (New Jersey) *Daily Times* reported that they and the city police were "swamped" with hundreds of phone calls and that "Near panic swept over some families in this city, as it did throughout other sections of the nation."[119] It was so convincing that it also resulted in what could be described as an outcry for punitive actions, FCC regulations, and an eventual apology from the producer, Orson Welles. Granted, the episode aired in the early days of World War II when global tensions were rising and were characterized by routine interruptions of your favorite radio show by news from the European front, and Americans were intently trying to stay abreast of the latest developments in Europe.

---

119 Chris Brock, "Sidebar: 'War of Worlds' Broadcast Caused Local Worry but Panic Overstated," Arts and Entertainment | Nny360.Com., 2020, http://web.archive.org/web/20220227024905/https://www.nny360.com/artsandlife/artsandentertainment/sidebar-war-of-worlds-broadcast-caused-local-worry-but-panic-overstated/article_694adb5b-2707-5501-a5e8-a16e1c73794b.html.

Nonetheless, this incident also displays how easily we can be misled. In the *New York Tribune*, Dorothy Thompson, a journalist who was also one of the first to express concerns about Adolph Hitler, pointed out America's susceptibility to propaganda when she wrote, "Mr. Orson Welles and *The Mercury Theater of the Air* have made one of the most fascinating demonstrations of all time. They have proved that a few effective voices, accompanied by sound effects, can convince masses of people of a totally unrealistic, completely fantastic proposition to create a nationwide panic."[120]

The third thing you should know about the UFO phenomenon is that we earthlings are gullible and easily deceived.

The Hoaxers and Close Encounter Wannabes Are Out There

The truth is out there, but sometimes it simply takes years to come out, if ever. We must be mindful that some UFO reports are the result of intentional hoaxes, scammers, and pranksters, yet some choose to believe in alien origins regardless of the facts. In November 1987, the *Gulf Breeze Sentinel* published a series of UFO photos sent to them by a local resident identifying himself as

120 Dorothy Thompson, "Mr. Welles and Mass Delusion," New York Herald Tribune, 1938, https://rwoconne.github.io/rwoclass/astr1210/welles-and-mass-delusion-DThompson-1938.html.

"Mr. X," resulting in worldwide attention for the small Florida town of approximately 5,000 residents.[121] Mr. X was later identified as Ed Walters, a local resident who claimed that in addition to the photos he'd taken, he had also been visited by the aliens operating the spacecraft.[122] Mutual UFO Network (MUFON) investigated the incident and was initially convinced of the authenticity of his photos and encounters.[123] Craig Myers, a reporter for the *Pensacola News Journal*, however, was skeptical.

His suspicions were confirmed three years later when a Styrofoam model of the Gulf Breeze UFO was discovered in the attic by the new owners of Walter's home. Myers was even able to duplicate the photos Walters had submitted.[124] Some groups, such as the Center for UFO Studies (CUFOS), concurred that Walter's photos had been hoaxed. Even the *National Enquirer* passed on purchasing his photos. Walters claimed that the model had been planted in the attic to discredit him and the Close Encounter Wannabes rushed to his defense.[125]

121 Wikipedia Contributors, "Gulf Breeze UFO Incident," Wikipedia, The Free Encyclopedia. 2022, https://en.wikipedia.org/wiki/Gulf_Breeze_UFO_incident.

122 Troy Moon, "Gulf Breeze UFO Sightings: 30 Years Later, Public Still Divided," Pensacola News Journal, 2017, https://www.pnj.com/story/news/2017/12/10/gulf-breeze-ufo-sightings-30-years-public-divided/915397001/.

123 Ibid.

124 Myers, Craig R. 2006. *War of the Words: The True but Strange Story of the Gulf Breeze UFO*. Xlibris.

125 Wikipedia Contributors, "Gulf Breeze UFO Incident," 2022.

In 2017, the *Pensacola News Journal* published an article entitled *Gulf Breeze UFO Phenomenon: 30 years later, sightings still divide the public*, demonstrating that there are some who don't want to be bothered by the facts.[126] Although there are plenty of other ambiguous and unexplainable UFO encounters, there will always be a segment of those within the UFO phenomenon who refuse to allow the facts, even staged hoaxes to adjust their beliefs on a particular incident. *The wise adjust their beliefs based upon the facts, but the unwise adjust the truth to accommodate their beliefs—even hoaxes.*

The "Alien Autopsy" film is another example of this element within the UFO phenomenon. Broadcast around the nation on cable and across the world on satellite, *The Alien Autopsy: Fact or Fiction* (spoiler alert: it's fiction) film took hoaxes to a new level and even exceeded the coverage that was given to the "Gulf Breeze" sightings. The seventeen-minute film, presented to look like grainy black and white footage from 1947, claimed to show the autopsy of an alien being from a crashed UFO outside of Roswell, N.M., now known as the *Roswell Incident*. Narration provided by actor Jonathan Frakes from *Star Trek: The Next Generation* aided in giving it some apparent credibility. Qualified experts in the field of autopsy, special effects, and film were quick to label it a hoax, but their voices fell on deaf ears. In 2006, a British special-

---

126 Moon, 2017.

effects creator, John Humphreys, claimed that he played a key role in the alien's creation and the film's producer, Ray Santilli, admitted that the film was a reproduction of the original he had seen in 1992 that he believed to be real but had no way of confirming.[127] So, to clarify, the producer admitted that it was a staged re-enactment. Nevertheless, some within the UFO community still cite it as proof of the Roswell crash and ET life. Earthlings are gullible.

Urban legends are birthed from repeated bits of false information that are repeated so frequently they are presumed to be the truth. *Some* are a blend of urban legend and/or suspect credentials. For example, one of the more famous UFO incidents involving a commercial airliner known as the *Alaska Incident* (which even has its own Wikipedia page[128]) is regularly cited as proof of ET.

For nearly fifty minutes on November 17, 1986, Japan Airlines Flight #1628 was reportedly approached by three UFOs over Alaska. Captain Kenju Terauchi said, "The thing was flying as if there was no such thing as gravity. It sped up, then stopped, then flew at our speed, in our direction, so that to us it [appeared to be] stand-

---

127 Nathalie Lagerfeld, "How an Alien Autopsy Hoax Captured the World's Imagination for a Decade," Time, 2016, https://time.com/4376871/alien-autopsy-hoax-history/.

128 Wikipedia Contributors, "Alaska Airlines Flight 261," Wikipedia, The Free Encyclopedia, 2022, https://en.wikipedia.org/wiki/Alaska_Airlines_Flight_261.

ing still. The next instant, it changed course."[129] However, crafts of the description given by Terauchi were not visible to a United Airlines crew nor to a military plane which were within the same area. This, of course, doesn't negate the presence of a UFO within the area, but what you'll probably never hear is that in addition to this particular *Alaska Incident*, Captain Terauchi had previously made *four* other UFO reports leading one to question if he's a "Close Encounter Wannabe".[130] Sure, lighting does indeed strike in the same place twice and, in some rare cases, even the same person, but why is it that some people seem to see UFOs more frequently than others?

Although multiple UFO sightings by one person may create suspicion, one surprising element of the phenomena is that it's not completely unusual for some people to have multiple credible sightings. Nevertheless, in addition to those who may instantly ascribe an unfamiliar aeronautical or cosmic event as evidence for ETI, some fall prey to their vivid imaginations and wishful thinking.

Vivid Imaginations and Wishful Thinking

Percival Lowell, a Harvard graduate with a distinction in mathematics and an elected "fellow" of the

---

129 "JAL Pilot's UFO Story Surfaces after 20 Years," UFO Casebook Files, Accessed April 22, 2022, https://www.ufocasebook.com/jal1628surfaces.html.

130 Ibid.

American Academy of Arts and Sciences, was a trained astronomer and credited with laying the groundwork resulting in the discovery of Pluto.[131] Although part of Lowell's theory that the solar system contained planets beyond Neptune (assuming Pluto is defined as a planet), his certainty of Martian-built canals was proven invalid. But because of the appearance of grooves on the surface of Mars and Lowell's desperate desire to prove that life existed there, he proceeded to draw diagrams and maps of canals that supported his theory, albeit incorrectly.[132] The same can happen to the best of good-natured people who are convinced beyond reason that every ancient structure, petroglyph, unexplained aerial phenomena, etc., is evidence of ET life. We, too, can be misled or diverted by wishful thinking and inaccurate information.

In more recent times, residents of Foshan in China's Guangdong province were alarmed when they observed what appeared to be a floating city in the clouds. The phenomenon lasted only a few minutes, and because there's only one known video of the incident, it very well may be a digital hoax. "If it is real, it's called a superior mirage, which just means it's an upward projecting mirage,' says Jill Coleman, an atmospheric scientist at Ball

131 Percival Lowell, *Mars and Its Canals* (New York: The Macmillian Company, 1906).

132 Ibid.

State University in Muncie, Indiana. It could be something called a 'fata morgana,' she says, which is a certain kind of atmospheric mirage."[133]

The incident generated discussions of the use of 3D holographic images, lasers, sounds, and projections into the clouds or sky for military use, communication, or *other* purposes. It's the concept of projecting virtual reality into the real world—without the goggles. There are countless rabbit holes and conspiracy theories regarding this concept, but the premise that humans can be deceived by technology is an established fact, and we shouldn't be shocked when we see technology being utilized for experimental and nefarious purposes. If Americans can be misled to the point of panic by a dramatized version of *War of the Worlds* in 1938 using radio, how might we see this historical event repeating itself in the future?

Without a doubt, we cannot dismiss the fact that credible people are indeed seeing things and having encounters that cannot currently be explained and for which there is seemingly no rational explanation, but in some cases, they are simply the side effects of our gullibility or wishful thinking, i.e., Close Encounter Wannabes. This, too, is an aspect of the UFO phenomenon, and *I predict that we'll see technology being used in*

---

133 Jane Lee, "China's Floating City and The Science of Mirages," National Geographic, 2015, https://www.nationalgeographic.com/science/article/151020-city-sky-china-mirage-fata-morgana-weather-atmosphere.

new and unforeseen ways to deceive people into believing we are being visited by ETCs. So, what about the unexplained phenomena?

CHAPTER 4

Close Encounters Are Bad for Your Health

Such advanced aliens would perhaps become
nomads, looking to conquer and colonize
whatever planets they could reach.

—Stephen Hawking

I remember watching a *Twilight Zone* re-run entitled
To Serve Man, in which a news conference had been
called by the Secretary General of the United Nations,
who proceeded to announce the arrival of aliens landing on earth. The alien ambassador announced that
the extraterrestrials had come to earth on what could
be described as a humanitarian mission that would
end famine and war, as well as provide free energy to
everyone on the planet. As a ceremonial gift, the alien

spokesman provided a book entitled *To Serve Man* to the delegation.[134]

Most people were elated by this development and eagerly offered their allegiance, cooperation, and acceptance. However, a young woman who was translating the entirety of the book from the alien's language to English discerned that the book was actually a cookbook—how to serve mankind as a dish you'd see on a restaurant menu—not a book on social justice.[135] The closing remarks of the episode refer to humanity going from being the rulers of a planet to an ingredient in someone's soup.

Childhood's End is a science fiction novel by Arthur C. Clarke in which the earth has been peacefully invaded by an alien race known as the Overlords, who rule by proxy but offer a promised paradise in return.[136] The "paradise" provided by the Overlords comes with a price: the slow but certain removal of human identity and culture. Only a select few people are allowed to actually see and interact with the Overlords, who were what could be described in the Bible as fallen angels. Although both examples are from 1950s science fiction, there's reason to believe that there are indeed some elements of truth

134 Wikipedia Contributors, "To Serve Man (The Twilight Zone) - Wikipedia." Wikipedia, The Free Encyclopedia, 2022, https://en.wikipedia.org/wiki/To_Serve_Man_(The_Twilight_Zone).

135 ibid.

136 Arthur C. Clarke, *Childhood's End*, Del Ray, 1953.

within these examples that may also be components of the UFO phenomenon.

Although more people than ever before believe that earth is being regularly visited by ETs, there isn't a clear answer within the UFO community as to why. Why would intelligent biological beings traverse the galaxies (or send technological hybrids in their place) to visit us for the purpose of administering unwanted proctology exams? How many more do they need to do?

Among other theories, some suggest that earth has been declared a cosmological preserve by other ETCs, or like zoologists, they seek to observe us in our natural habitat. Other theories propose that they want to help evolve humanity, protect us from destroying ourselves, or that they're scouting us out for the purpose of eventually invading us. For years Stephen Hawking expressed his view that making contact with intelligent extraterrestrials would be very detrimental to humanity, describing them as cosmic nomads that would conquer any inferior civilizations they encountered.[137] In film and literature, characters are defined by their actions. In many ways, that can be said of all of us, and I believe the principle applies to ETs as well. Although the paranormal has become normal, the aspect that is generally overlooked by mainstream America is the devious

137 Calla Cofield, "Stephen Hawking: Intelligent Aliens Could Destroy Humanity, But Let's Search Anyway," Space, 2015, https://www.space.com/29999-stephen-hawking-intelligent-alien-life-danger.html.

and malevolent nature of aliens and abductions. Let's consider the following:

Animals

It's no secret that dogs have incredible senses. Some reports seem to show that they can even detect health issues in people around them. Their sense of smell and ability to hear high frequencies make them sensitive to certain things that humans are not. Other members of the animal kingdom can sense impending earthquakes and approaching storms from hundreds of miles away. Others can discern the earth's magnetic north without the aid of a compass.

The Book of Numbers records an unusual event in which a donkey is able to see an angel, whereas its rider is oblivious to the being's presence (Numbers 22:23–27). Therefore, it is not too far of a stretch to believe that the animal kingdom might be able to have a sense for the supernatural. Dr. Hugh Ross said, "Animals, especially dogs, cattle, and horses, have shown noticeable agitation in the presence of UFOs. Animals and pets have reportedly reacted to the presence of UFOs *before* their human observers (...). In some cases, incessant barking and mooing occurred before, during, and after the sighting. In other cases, dogs reportedly cowered and refused to go outside at the time of a UFO event, and

cattle herds stampeded."[138] UFO encounters in an area
are often preceded by the unusual silence of both animals and even insects. It's as if even animals and crick-
ets know there's something unsafe within the vicinity;
sadly, this is especially the case for cows.

Cattle and Livestock Mutilations

Cattle and livestock mutilations have been around
for a while, with the first known documented case being reported in 16th century England in an article saying, "Whole slaughters of sheep have been made, in
some places to number 100, in others less, where nothing is taken from the sheep but their tallow and some
inward parts, the whole carcasses, and fleece remaining
still behind."[139]

The animal mutilation phenomena (generally cattle)
are composed of several odd common denominators,
with the most notable being that blood has been drained
from the animals; these animals had not exhibited any
health issues or concerns the day before the mutilation.
In addition to the eyes, the reproductive organs have often been removed, and scavengers generally avoid the
carcasses. There are no tracks (human, animal, other)

138 Hugh Ross, Kenneth Samples, and Mark Clark, *Lights in the Sky &*
Little Green Men, (Colorado Springs: CO: NavPress Publishing Group), 68.

139 Christopher O'Brien, *Stalking the Herd: Unraveling the Cattle Mutila-*
tion Mystery, (Kempton, IL: Adventures Unlimited Press, 2014), 50.

in the immediate vicinity of the animal. Make no mistake, cattle and other livestock are being mutilated.

From April to August of 1975, over sixty cattle mutilations were reported in Colorado alone.[140] When ranchers report these mutilations, there's a consensus that something bizarre had happened, but no one was ever prosecuted. Although some law enforcement agencies suggest that the animals are being mutilated by unidentified religious cults, generally speaking, no charges were filed because they simply don't know who to blame or charge.

Strangely, these mutilations are often preceded by reports of UFOs, black helicopters, and on some occasions, the appearance of strange unidentifiable creatures. The gruesome cattle and livestock remains are examples of physical evidence of something very nefarious and evil in nature. These mutilations, I might add, are also very real to the ranchers and owners of the cattle, which have experienced an appalling death and dissection at the hands of their perpetrators, not to mention the financial loss to the owners. On August 14, 2021, the Thomas Angus Ranch (Oregon) reported the loss and mutilation of a prized Black Angus bull valued

---

140 Heidi Beedle, "Colorado's Cattle Mutilation History and the Journalist Who Wouldn't Let It Go," Colorado Springs Indy, 2019, https://www. csindy.com/temporary_news/colorado-s-cattle-mutilation-history-and-the-journalist-who-wouldn-t-let-it-go/article_6769e632-2de0-5997-beda-9e12f9088bea.html.

at $4,500.[141] As usual, the reproductive organs had been removed with exceptionally precise surgical cuts.[142]

If you've ever seen any interviews on cattle mutilations, it probably included Linda Moulton Howe, a Stanford-educated reporter who is often consulted for any program that's discussing the topic. Having researched over 1,000 livestock mutilation cases and being the executive producer of a documentary entitled *A Strange Harvest: Further Evidence Linking Animal Mutilations and Human Abductions to Alien Life Forms*, she's easily an expert on the topic who's often interviewed and consulted for any show or documentary covering animal mutilations. Interestingly, she concludes that extra-terrestrials are the most likely culprit.[143] [144] Christopher O'Brien, author of *Stalking the Herd: Unraveling the Cattle Mutilation Mystery*, suggests that "extra-terrestrials [are] possibly trying to learn about humans through cows. Cattle hemoglobin, the oxygen-carrying protein in red blood cells,

141 Sierra Dawn McClaim, "Mysterious Cattle Mutilations Continue in Central and Eastern Oregon," Capital Press, 2021, https://www.capitalpress.com/ag_sectors/livestock/mysterious-cattle-mutilations-continue-in-central-and-eastern-oregon/article_47e16326-0537-11ec-a50e-c7abb8e5e93e.html.

142 Ibid.

143 Community History Writers, "No Mention of Satanic Cults – or UFO's – in CBI Report," The Fort Morgan Times, 2018, https://www.fortmorgantimes.com/2018/11/05/no-mention-of-satanic-cults-or-ufos-in-cbi-report/.

144 Linda Moulton Howe, *A Strange Harvest* (TV Movie 1980) – IMDb, https://www.imdb.com/title/tt6362274/.

is nearly an exact match with that found in people."[145] Due to the fact that the reproductive organs are often removed, it would seem that some type of research is being done in an effort to learn about, and possibly replicate, some form of biological life. However, these perpetrators are not only researching and experimenting on animals but also on humans.

Abductions

In 1975, a group of loggers in the vicinity of Snowflake, Arizona observed an unidentifiable bright light in the sky that was hovering just below tree line. Attempting to get a better view, one of the loggers, Travis Walton, was "abducted" and disappeared for five days.[146] In this case, there were six eyewitnesses who'd seen Walton being knocked over by a beam of light that was directed at him from a UFO hovering just under the tree line.[147] Walton's coworkers initially fled for their lives and to get help but then realized that they couldn't abandon him and chose to return to the scene of the incident. By the time they returned, he was nowhere

145 Joseph Rose, "UFOs, Mutilated Cows and Oregon: What's the Link?" The Oregonian: Oregon Live, 2016, https://www.oregonlive.com/entertainment/2016/02/ufo_cow_mutilations_oregon_no.html.

146 Travis Walton, The Walton Experience (New York: Berkley Pub. Corp., 1978).

147 Wikipedia Contributors, "Travis Walton UFO Incident," Wikipedia, The Free Encyclopedia, 2022, https://en.wikipedia.org/wiki/Travis_Walton_UFO_incident.

to be found. Due to the failure of local authorities in locating Walton, his coworkers were even suspected of foul play, possibly murder.

After five days, Walton woke up face down and made his way back to civilization, where he placed a collect phone call from a payphone in Heber, Arizona, to his family. As a form of therapy, he journaled his account, which was later published in 1979 under the title "The Walton Experience"[148] and was subsequently made into a film, *Fire in the Sky*, fifteen years later.

In 2022 I met with Travis Walton in Snowflake, Arizona. He was very kind, gracious, unassuming, well-read, intelligent, likable, a bit shy, and down to earth, whom I would describe as a very reluctant UFO celebrity. He was very matter-of-fact about his encounter. I felt as if I somewhat looked into his soul and have no doubt that he experienced an abduction. Walton believes that the beings "abducted" him because they were concerned about his physical welfare after being struck by the beam.[149] However, both then and now, he described it as a horrific experience that was conducted against his will. When I asked him if he would have done anything differently, he said, "I would've never gotten out of the truck."[150]

---

148 Walton, 1978.

149 Travis Walton, Interviewed by the Author, Snowflake, AZ, March 28, 2022.

150 Ibid.

Aside from Walton, one of the most famous abduction encounters is now known as the *Hill Abduction*, in which Barney and Betty Hill claimed they were abducted by aliens "in a rural portion of New Hampshire on September 19, 1961. It was the first widely publicized report of an alien abduction in the United States."[151] [152] There were several fascinating aspects of their abduction. In addition to unaccounted for missing time, Betty was able to reproduce a hand-drawn map of what seems to be the Zeta Reticuli star system that she said was shown to her by aliens after inquiring about their origin.[153] [154] Additionally, she said that the aliens inserted a needle into her navel, cut off a lock of her hair, and kept her fingernail trimmings and some skin flakes.[155]

However, one particularly unusual aspect of abductions is the fascination ETs have with human sexuality. Barney Hill later added that the aliens had also collected his sperm during their abduction. During an interview with Shane Hurd of MUFON Arizona, I asked him what his oddest case was, and although he was unable to confirm nor deny the veracity of the report, he stated that

151 Wikipedia Contributors, "Barney and Betty Hill," Wikipedia, The Free Encyclopedia, 2022, https://en.wikipedia.org/wiki/Barney_and_Betty_Hill.

152 Brookesmith, 1995.

153 Ibid.

154 Jacques Vallee, *Messengers of Deception: UFO Contacts and Cults* (Daily Grail Publishing, 2008).

155 Wikipedia Contributors, "Barney and Betty Hill," 2022.

on one occasion, a woman had reported that she'd been "raped" during an abduction.[156] In some cases, it even appears that there's a family history with UFOs and abductions, suggesting that they are monitoring particular genetic lines and favor those with green eyes and a particular blood type (Rh-negative).

The vast majority of UFO abduction encounters are *not* pleasant and wholesome experiences for the abductee. Whitley Strieber said, "I felt an absolutely indescribable sense of menace."[157] For the most part, these are nightmarish events that often plague the victims for years, if not the rest of their lives. Negative side effects always seem to accompany those who experience a close encounter of the fourth kind (i.e., the person is taken aboard a craft and experimented upon), with some reporting not only radiation sickness, nausea, and nightmares but also unexplainable scratches and scars; a characteristic that's often associated with demonic possession.

Dr. David Jacobs, who served as an associate professor of history at Temple University, a pioneer in the abduction element of the UFO phenomena, has perhaps conducted more case studies than anyone in the field and provides the following account:

156 Anonymous, Interviewed by the Author, Fountain Hills, March 5, 2022.

157 Whitley Strieber, *Transformation: The Breakthrough* (New York: William Morrow & Co., 1988).

Allison Reed was twenty-eight when she called me in June of 1993. She and her husband operated a successful home-based business. She reached me while my family and I were on vacation on Long Beach Island, New Jersey. She was worried about odd things that had been happening to her throughout her life. She had learned to cope with them silently, but now her eight-year-old son and five-year-old daughter had been telling her of strange and frightening things happening to them, too. She grew increasingly alarmed as her children's descriptions of their experiences seemed to be confirmed by physical marks on their bodies.[158]

Although generally composed of earthly elements such as iron, which have a similar composition to meteorites, some abductees report that they acquired implants as a result of their abduction. These unexplainable pieces of metal can be viewed by X-rays and have been physically removed by surgeons.[159] Several authors such as Dr. David Jacobs, Dr. Roger Leir, Dr. John E.

---

158 David M. Jacobs, *The Threat: Revealing the Secret Alien Agenda* (New York: Simon & Schuster, 1999), 23.

159 David M. Jacobs, *Walking Among Us: The Alien Plan to Control Humanity* (New York: Disinformation Books, 2015).

Mack, and investigator Derrel Sims have addressed and documented this phenomenon. Jacques Valle, a pioneer in objectively researching UFOs, said, "The experience of a close encounter with a UFO is a shattering physical and mental ordeal. The trauma has effects that go far beyond what the witnesses recall consciously. New types of behavior are conditioned, and new types of beliefs are promoted."[160]

The fourth thing you should know about the UFO phenomenon is that Close Encounters can be bad for your health.

On a purely personal note, it would make sense that if a benevolent extraterrestrial civilization would go through the dangers and trouble of traversing light-years of time and space to reach Earth that they would at least provide us with something beneficial, such as a cure for a disease or provide insights for lessening the dangers of space travel.

In an interview on the topic of whether or not aliens would intervene in human affairs to prevent World War III, Nick Pope pointed out: "Even if we're being observed by benign extraterrestrials, they didn't intervene to stop atomic bombs being dropped on Hiroshima or Nagasaki, so there's no reason to suppose they'd intervene

---

160 Valle, 2008, 8–9.

to stop a nuclear war now. Frankly, it's a spiritual belief that reminds me of religion, with its central premise of salvation from above."[161]

So far, the extraterrestrials have provided absolutely nothing to improve humanity's condition. There have been no new cures, no new medical technologies, and not even an autographed space map. Rather, they seem content with kidnapping people against their will (i.e., abductions), administrating unwanted physicals, sexual assault, mutilating cattle, and preaching New Age doctrines of evolution and pluralism. These are not the activities of benevolent creatures concerned about climate change but are the characteristics you'd expect from those with malevolent purposes.

As seen in the Bible, the forces of darkness (demons and fallen angels) seek to torment and destroy humanity. Those who are possessed are being systematically destroyed. In one case, a demon-possessed man is reported to be regularly cutting himself (Mark 5:5), and in another, a boy is being influenced to drown himself or to throw himself into a fire (Mark 9:22). The ministry of Jesus, on the other hand, regularly involved the casting out of demons, demonstrating His power over the spirit world (e.g., Luke 11:14–23). Paul references un-

---

161 Frank Chung, "Russia Ukraine: UFO Believers Think Aliens Will Stop Nuclear WW3," Nation Wide News, 2022, https://www.news.com.au/technology/science/space/ufo-believers-think-aliens-will-stop-nuclear-war/news-story/133ae70c82dfb22119ed79bfbb400e36.

holy, non-human, intelligent beings described as powers, thrones, dominions, and principalities (Ephesians 6:12, Colossians 1:15–17), even warning us that since not all are benevolent, we should put on the full armor of God (Ephesians 6:10), indicating that they can affect the physical world. This reference affirms that they are a real threat and that we are at a disadvantage without the referenced armor of God. Please read on.

CHAPTER 5

Extraterrestrial or Interdimensional

Yet across the gulf of space, minds that are to
our minds as ours are to those of the beasts
that perish, intellects vast and cool and un-
sympathetic, regarded this earth with envi-
ous eyes, and slowly and surely drew their
plans against us.

—H.G. Wells, *War of the Worlds*

Dr. John Mack, a Pulitzer-Prize winning author and
professor of psychiatry at Harvard University, who'd examined just under a hundred abduction cases, astutely
observed that UFOs "seem to partake of properties be-
longing to both the spirit and material worlds, bridging,
as if effortlessly, the division between these realms..."[162]
UFOs seem to be like the episode five version of Obi-

---

162 John Mack, *Abduction: Human Encounters with Aliens* (New York:
Scribner, 1994), 404-405.

Wan Kenobi from *Star Wars* in that they appear out of nowhere, make a few comments, and then disappear without a trace. Unlike other cosmic objects, satellites, comets, etc., they cannot be tracked for any length of time. Rather, UFOs often seem to disappear as quickly as they appear, like an apparition and at will, suggesting that they are not traveling from another galaxy but rather another dimension... the spiritual dimension.

The Book of 2 Kings, Chapter 6, records an interesting scene in which Elisha and his servant are surrounded by enemy forces. Things are not looking good for them, and the servant is understandably fearful of the circumstances. Elisha prays that his servant's eyes may be opened. God answers this prayer, and we're told that chariots of fire—the army of God—were also present. Interestingly, God's army was there but simply imperceivable to the naked eye. In Luke's account of the first Christmas, he records that the announcement of Christ's birth to the "shepherds keeping watch over their flocks by night" (Luke 2:8 ESV) is made by an angel of the Lord with instructions as to where to find the newborn King. Luke then reports, "And *suddenly* there was with *the* angel a *multitude* of the heavenly host praising God and saying, 'Glory to God in the highest, and on earth peace among those with whom He is pleased!'" (Luke 2:13–14 ESV, emphasis mine). It appears that, like Elisha's scenario, the angels were there the whole time, and yet their presence was not manifested until after the angel had given the announcement and pertinent details.

Physicist Jacques Lematre, author of the somewhat classic (in UFO circles) *Flying Saucer Review* said, "We can consequently conclude that it is impossible to interpret the UFO phenomenon in terms of material spaceships as we conceive of the latter, i.e., in terms of manufactured, self-propelled machines retaining their material nature and their mechanical structure to travel from one solar system to another by traversing the distance separating these systems in the Einsteinian Continuum."[163] In 1979, UFO researcher Jacques Vallee said, "The UFO phenomenon represents a manifestation of a reality that transcends our current understanding of physics."[164] Consider that UFOs generate no sonic booms when they break the sound barrier, nor do they seem to have any issues with air resistance. They may be detected by radar but not seen by pilots and vice versa. They leave no heat signatures, nor is there any evidence of their propulsion system.

Nick Redfern has written scores of articles and books on UFOs and serves as a consultant on the topic of programs featured on the *Discovery* and *History* channels. On his website, "Mysterious Universe," he said,

---

163 Charles Bowen ed., *Flying Saucer Review - Vol. 15, N. 6: November-December 1969 (FSR)*, Flying Saucer Service LTD, 1968, 23.

164 Valle, 1979, 209-210.

> Back when I was in my twenties, I was of the
> opinion that UFOs were extraterrestrial (...) As
> I slid into my thirties, however, my thoughts
> slowly began to change (something which
> also happened for a few friends of mine in the
> field, too) (...) my views—today—are far closer
> to those suggested by John Keel. Namely, that
> we're dealing with something that co-exists
> with us and masquerades as ET.[165]

The "Condon Report" (aka "The Condon Committee"
or the *Scientific Study of Unidentified Flying Objects*), conducted by the University of Colorado and funded by the
U.S. Air Force between 1966 and 1968, concluded that
further study of UFOs would not yield any scientific
discoveries.[166] The *Condon Report* examined hundreds of
selected files from *Project Blue Book*, the National Investigations Committee on Aerial Phenomenon, and the
Aerial Phenomena Research Organization, including
radar and visual reports and those made by astronauts,
concluded in 14,855 pages that further study of UFOs
would not yield any scientific advancements. However,

165 Nick Redfern, "UFOs: Extraterrestrial? Probably Not," Mysterious
Universe, 2016, https://mysteriousuniverse.org/2016/04/ufos-extraterres-
trial-probably-not/.

166 Edward U. Condon. "Scientific Study of Unidentified Flying Objects
By the University of Colorado Under Contract N. 44620-67-C with the
United States Air Force," 1968, www.ncas.org.

there were several insightful revelations, one of which said, "It all but demolished the idea that Earth was being visited by creatures from other planets and galaxies."[167] Basically, it concluded that there was no hard evidence to conclude that UFOs and their occupants were beings from other planets or galaxies but that "their occupants should be attributed to paraphysical phenomena."[168] "Paraphysical" is defined by Merriam-Webster as something "resembling physical phenomena but without recognizable physical cause,"[169] meaning that extraterrestrials and their crafts can at the very least appear, if not take on a solid form.

The "Tic Tac" UFO was able to go from 80,000 feet to 50,000 feet in less than a second; furthermore, it arrived at the classified rendezvous point before the military vessels involved in the exercise as if to say, "I know your plans." If you were mentally able to subtract the spaceship factor from the UFO phenomena, you'd notice that it has most, if not all, of the same characteristics of a haunted house. By this, I'm implying that both UFOs and poltergeists are able to materialize and dematerialize at will. In addition to being able to pass through walls in abduction accounts, they can also change their shape, size, color, and communicate by telepathy (or

---

167 Ibid.

168 Ibid.

169 "Paraphysical," In *Merriam-Webster Online Dictionary*. Merriam-Webster, Incorporated, 2022, https://www.merriam-webster.com/dictionary/paraphysical.

channeling). They can move physical objects, produce tangible impressions in the ground and on people, and appear to have a very physical form, including the ability to be photographed and have their image captured on film.

As J. Allen Hynek said, "We must wonder where UFOs are 'hiding' when not manifesting themselves to human eyes."[170] On the television or movie screen, spacecraft are free to fly without any limitations except those of their creator's imagination. When UFOs are pursued by military aircraft, not only are they outmaneuvered, but in most cases, the crafts simply disappear. Despite that, in the real and tangible world, the laws of physics are still applicable, at least to that which is physical. UFOs, however, disobey firmly established physical laws. Likewise, they only reveal themselves on their terms. What exactly are they?

Angels: Holy and Unholy

The fifth thing you should know about UFOs is that they exhibit the capabilities of interdimensional travel, like angels.

The Bible reveals that there are spiritual creatures referred to as angels that could be classified as extra-

170 J. Allen Hynek, (Joseph Allen), Philip J. Klass, and Jacques Vallee, *The Edge of Reality: A Progress Report on Unidentified Flying Objects* (Chicago, IL: Henry Regnery Co., 1967), 12-13.

terrestrial in the sense that, unlike Adam and Eve, their origins are not earthly, and they predate humanity and earth itself.

> "Where were you when I laid the founda-
> tion of the earth? Tell me, if you possess un-
> derstanding! Who set its measurements—if
> you know—or who stretched a measuring
> line across it? On what were its bases set, or
> who laid its cornerstone—when the **morning
> stars** sang in chorus, and all the **sons of God**
> shouted for joy?"
> (Job 38:4–7 NET, emphasis mine)

Regarding its authorship and time of composition, many Bible commentators consider Job to be the oldest book of the Bible and that the events recorded therein occurred before the Exodus—possibly much earlier. The "morning stars" and "sons of God" are classes of angels who've been around longer than humanity. Whereas there's only one human race, we see that there are many types of humans. God could've created just one type of tree, but there are all types of trees. Simply put, God is very creative, and He likes variety. The same is true of the angels, some of which, if not all, holy and unholy, possess the ability to travel between dimensions.

There are those who believe that Ezekiel's wheels are an example of the ability of angels to travel between dimensions and to take passengers with them. "The Lord lifted Ezekiel up, taking him on the first known aerial tour, showing him sights from his own era. Finally, he was taken to the future, manipulating time as easily as we move from one place to another in our familiar destination."[171] This material sounds sensational, yet the evidence for the origins of aliens being interdimensional (angelic) is much more plausible than an ETC one, and when you take into consideration that on one account, Jesus and the disciples were instantly transported to their destination (John 6:21) as was Philip following the baptism of the Ethiopian eunuch (Acts 8:39–40), "spiritual" teleportation through time and space has biblical support. Dr. John Mack said, "Quite a few abductees have spoken to me of their sense that at least some of their experiences are not occurring within the physical space-time dimensions of the universe as we comprehend it."[172]

When holy angels are dispatched by God to communicate with humans, they sometimes appear in human form. Could unholy angels be dispatched by Satan to communicate with humans in a non-human, alien form? Yes. What then is their purpose and agenda?

---

171 Gary Stearman, *Time Travelers of the Bible: How Hebrew Prophets Shattered the Barriers of Time and Space* (Oklahoma City: Blessed Hope Publishing, 2014), 228.

172 John E. Mack, *Abduction: Human Encounters with Aliens* (Scribner's, 1994), 402.

CHAPTER 6

Wolves in Extraterrestrial Clothing

Beloved, do not believe every spirit, but test the spirits to see whether they are from God, for many false prophets have gone out into the world. By this you know the Spirit of God: every spirit that confesses that Jesus Christ has come in the flesh is from God, and every spirit that does not confess Jesus is not from God. This is the spirit of the antichrist, which you heard was coming and now is in the world already.

(1 John 4:1–3 ESV)

In The *Phoenix Lights*, author Dr. Lynne Kitei begins by sharing that her spiritual journey included researching Edgar Cayce and near-death experiences and that she even, for lack of a better word, prayed to the entities to provide her with revelation regarding their purpose.[173] This could be described as conjuring. Shane Hurd, a field investigator in Phoenix for MUFON, said, "Because of their spiritual nature, I personally don't investigate orbs," and informed me that there was a special branch of MUFON dedicated to investigating the spiritual and paranormal aspects of the phenomena.[174] The fact that spirituality is a common denominator of the UFO phenomenon is one of its best-kept secrets.

If you follow the trail of the UFO phenomena long enough, you'll discover that it's a trail that often ends up within the realm of Eastern religious beliefs, New Age, or the occult. In addition to reports of unaccounted time in abduction accounts, another interesting characteristic of close encounters of the third kind is that occult-like methods are sometimes employed to establish contact; many abductees describe that ESP or telepathy is utilized in their communication with the aliens. The religion of extraterrestrials is typically a version of New Age, which is actually very old. It's so old that it goes back to the Garden of Eden with the temptation to "be like God" (Genesis 3:5).

173 Lynne Kitei, *The Phoenix Lights* (Charlottesville, VA: Hampton Roads Publishing Co., 2004), 30, 159, 168, 170, and 203-208.

174 Shane Hurd, Interview with the Author, Fountain Hills, AZ, March 19, 2022.

There's a spiritual element within New Age circles that provides some familiarity, reassurance, and comfort to those who not only believe in ETs but also believe that they're on a benevolent mission in which they've come to save humanity through spiritual enlightenment; that is, they've come to show us a path to "godhood". In some cases, such as the Heaven's Gate cult, thirty-nine people committed mass suicide with the false hope of achieving this higher spiritual plane by being united with aliens.[175] Laura Magdalene Eisenhower, the great-granddaughter of President Dwight Eisenhower, a popular speaker in UFO circles, said that she is deeply connected to "Sophia," which she calls a divine feminine energy of love and wisdom.[176] In 2006 she claims to have been contacted by "Mars recruiters" but felt uncomfortable about their offer and since then has felt strange things going on around her, such as "cyclones of energy coming down around me even on sunny days."[177] She sees herself as an "ambassador to the unified field".

175 Laura Barcella, "Heaven's Gate, 25 Years Later: Remembering Lives Lost in Cult," People Weekly 2022, https://people.com/crime/heavens-gate-cult-suicide-remembering-lives-lost/.

176 Laura Magdalene Eisenhower, "SPIRIT REALITY Blog: Sophia," United Vibrations: Wordpress, Accessed May 16, 2022, https://unitedvibrations.wordpress.com/laura-magdalene-eisenhower/.

177 Mike Szymanski, "Eisenhower Great-Granddaughter Discusses Time Travel, Mars and ETs," Patch Media, 2012, https://patch.com/california/studiocity/eisenhower-great-granddaughter-discusses-time-travel-5503567164.

Although Guadalupe, Mexico, and Fatima, Portugal have become synonymous in most Roman Catholic circles for their reports of Marian apparitions, i.e., an appearance of the Virgin Mary, you may be surprised to know that since the fourth century, from France to Mexico, there have been hundreds, not scores, of Marian apparitions all over the world. One twentieth-century event that you may not have heard of took place in Medjugorje, Bosnia, just miles from the Croatian border, when on June 24, 1981, six children reported seeing a young woman with a child in her arms, who motioned them to come closer but being too afraid to do so they ran off in the opposite direction.[178] The next day, at the same time, four of them had the same encounter, but this time stated that they recognized her as the Virgin Mary. From that day forward, they reportedly had daily encounters resulting in people from around the world making "pilgrimages" there to have their own encounters.

At the insistence of some colleagues in the late 1980s, Dwight Longenecker made what could be described as a reluctant visit to Medjugorje, where he said that he had his own encounter. After praying the rosary for forty minutes, he said, "My friend nudged me in the ribs and pointed at the sky. I looked up to see that the sun hov-

---

178 "Medjugorje 41 Years of Apparitions," Foundation Marypages, Accessed May 16, 2022, https://www.marypages.com/medjugorje-(bosnia-and-herzegovina)-en.html.

ered in the sky like a white *disc* (emphasis mine) of light. The disc seemed to be spinning first clockwise and then counter-clockwise, while beams of light radiated from it like a spinning firework."[179]

I should add that there are thousands who report similar encounters in Medjugorje, not to mention Lourdes, France, Fatima, Portugal, etc. Whereas generally, the messages from these Marian apparitions are often generic, i.e., pray for peace, etc., oddly, the pilgrims are never exhorted to worship Jesus as God nor to seek forgiveness of their sins *through Jesus Christ*. If it really was Mary, she would most certainly tell people to worship Jesus, not her. Knowing the devil is "crafty" (Genesis 3:1), what better method to mislead the spiritually hungry with Roman Catholic roots than a Marian apparition? Crafty. Simply put, if it really were Mary, she would undoubtedly direct people to give glory to Jesus, not herself.

True and holy messengers of God will, like the holy angels of the Christmas story (Luke 2:8–14), always direct people to worship Jesus and no one else. Upon an angelic visit on the island of Patmos, John initially falls to his knees, but the holy angel immediately exhorts him to get to his feet.

---

179 Dwight Longenecker and David Gustafson, *Mary: A Catholic-Evangelical Debate* (Gracewing Publishing, 2003), 136.

I John, am the one who heard and saw these things. And when I heard and saw them, I fell down to worship at the feet of the angel who showed them to me, but he said to me, "You must not do that! I am a fellow servant with you and your brothers the prophets, and with those who keep the words of this book. Worship God."

(Revelation 22:8–9 ESV)

Writing to the church in Galatia, the Apostle Paul said, "But, even if we or an angel from heaven should preach a gospel other than the one we preached to you, let them be under God's curse. As we have said before, so now I say again: If anyone is preaching to you a gospel contrary to the one you received, let him be accursed" (Galatians 1:8–9 NIV). I can think of at least two religions whose founders claimed to have had angelic visitations. Perhaps, but if true they were not holy angels.

During the Cold War, a secret group within the U.S. Government was seeking to discover unconventional forms of warfare such as weaponizing the weather, ESP, mind control, and remote viewing. Another element of this was to establish contact with extraterrestrials *before* the communists.

The roots of the U.S. Government's interest in these topics seemingly stemmed from information suggesting that following World War II, the Soviets had acquired the occultic modus operandi that Hitler had been interested in weaponizing. An occultist and most-ly self-taught rocket scientist, Jack Parsons, who was employed by the Jet Propulsion Laboratory (JPL), was recruited to conduct research into making contact with ETs, which used what can only be described as sorcery and witchcraft. As far out and conspiratorial as this may seem, it has been confirmed by the CIA in a document released in 1977 entitled *Parapsychology in Intelligence* by Dr. Kenneth Kress that a group within the U.S. Government was secretly tasked and funded to investigate the validity of parapsychology and presumably, the para-normal.[180] Although it doesn't confirm the Collins Elite, nor can it be used to confirm the government's attempt to make contact with ETs, the document alludes to the government's interest in ESP, remote viewing, etc., for intelligence gathering. The report first appeared in a 1977 issue of "Studies in Intelligence," an internal publi-cation for the CIA made available to the public in 1996.[181]

According to Nick Redfern, a seasoned and objective researcher within the field of Ufology, one of the mem-bers of this research team was a Christian who identi-

---

180 Kenneth A. Kress, "Full Text of 'Parapsychology In Intelligence: A Personal Review and Conclusions' - Original Report 1977," Journal of Sci-entific Exploration, 1999, 13 (1). https://archive.org/stream/Parapsycholo-gyInIntelligence/Parapsychology-in-Intelligence_djvu.txt.

181 Ibid.

fied as a Quaker from Collins, New York, and the name
Collins Elite came about as the result of good-natured
ribbing from his peers on the team.[182] Their work, however, was very serious and sought to pick up where Jack
Parsons (an occultist) had left off due to a sudden, un-
timely, and I might add, unusual death. Before reading
any further, the following information about the Collins Elite is anecdotal, second-hand, and unable to be
verified at this time. However, what's interesting is that
the story is rooted in secular and not Christian sources.
That being said, as the story goes, upon investigation,
the Christian members (often described as "Fundamentalist Christians") within the *Collins Elite* were disturbed and alarmed not only by the occult practices required for making contact with the extraterrestrials but
deduced that the catalyst behind the UFO phenomenon
was demonic, resulting in their reluctance to investigate further via the methods utilized for establishing
contact.

Whitley Strieber based his best-selling book *Communion: A True Story* upon his personal abduction experience. I should inform you that he's also a horror author. Nonetheless, he describes his encounter by saying,
"Increasingly I felt as if I were entering a struggle that
might be even more than life and death. It might be a

---

182 Nick Redfern, *Final Events and the Secret Government Group on Demonic UFOs and the Afterlife* (San Antonio, TX: Anomalist Books, 2010),
41.

struggle for my soul, my essence, or whatever part of me might have reference to the eternal."[183] In this somewhat groundbreaking book, he said, "I'm 80% sure that (UFOs) are *visitors from another aspect of reality, not necessarily from another planet*" (emphasis mine).[184] He further speculates that they are "intelligent beings (...) goblins (...) or demons."[185] In an unpublished manuscript, Strieber said,

> In looking at the background of UFO abductees, it quickly became clear almost to a man, they have some background in New Age and occultic beliefs. Interestingly, studies show that there are very few practicing Christians or Jews amongst UFO contactees. What could this mean? Are aliens racist? Or does this, rather, indicate something about the belief systems of the abductees themselves?[186]

Of particular interest is that these beings who claim to have traversed time and space never seem to have

---

183 Whitley Strieber, *Transformation: The Breakthrough* (William Morrow & Co, 1988), 36.

184 Whitley Strieber and James Kunetka, *Communion: A True Story* (Beech Tree Books, 1987), 206.

185 Ibid, 207.

186 William M. Alnor, "UFO Cults Are Flourishing in New Age Circles," *Christian Research Journal* Summer, 1990, 5, https://christian.net/pub/resources/text/cri/cri-jrnl/web/crj0073a.html.

anything negative to say about Mohammed or Buddha, yet they seem to have a particular disdain for Jesus and Christianity. The predominant spokesmen (prophets) in America's "golden age" (the 1950s) of UFOs consisted of spokesmen like George Adamski, George Van Tassel, Desmond Leslie, Jack Parsons, William Pelley, and Brother Philip. All of them admitted to involvement with the occult, using telepathy, channeling, ESP, and the need to be in an altered state of consciousness for communicating with the ETs. In some cases, Ouija boards were utilized, and most of these "UFO prophets" were very influenced by the teachings of Aleister Crowley, who described himself as the "great beast" (cf. Revelation 13:1–8). A significant percentage of all alleged abductees have admitted to being involved in some form of cultic beliefs, practices, and even witchcraft. Whether knowingly or not, some may have invited the forces of darkness into their lives.

Spiritual Catfishing

In the online dating world, "catfishing" is a term used to describe those who create a very attractive persona, a false identity, on social media that doesn't really exist for relationships or other purposes. By using a more attractive photo and interesting biographical data, "catfish" lure people into a relationship on the premise of being someone they're not. In a similar fashion, the End

Times will be characterized by deception. Paul warned the Church in Galatia to beware of false teachings regardless of how impressive the source might be (Galatians 1:8), as did Jesus, who foretold of false prophets who would be able to perform wonders that, if possible, would deceive even the elect (Matthew 24:24).

Similarly, although there have been numerous reports of contact with aliens, thus far, none has yet to acknowledge Jesus Christ as *the* Son of God. So far, no "extraterrestrial" has led anyone to Christ or acknowledged God as their Creator. (If you know of any, please let me know about it). Rather, they almost always tend to repeat what could be described as New Age dogma.

Kenneth Arnold, who, after making a report of a UFO over Mt. Rainer, Washington, in 1947, can be credited with unwittingly creating the term "flying saucer," supposedly said in a radio interview that he was contacted by a Texas preacher who cautioned him that UFOs were "harbingers of doomsday."[187] Perhaps the unknown Texas preacher was right. Jesus warned that the birth pains of His return would be preceded by false prophets and signs in the heavens (Matthew 24:4–5, 11, 23–24, 29).

In an effort to mislead humanity away from Christ, these fallen angels are and will continue to masquerade and spiritually "catfish" as benevolent extraterrestrials

---

187 Jeff Smith, "Thinking Flashes in the Sky (Part 1)," San Diego Reader, 2013, https://www.sandiegoreader.com/news/2013/sep/11/unforgettable-thinking-flashes-sky-part-1/.

who've come to assist humanity in its darkest hour by offering false hope of unity through spiritual evolution by presenting themselves as humanity's creator. *The Last Battle*, the seventh and final of the *Chronicles of Narnia* by C.S. Lewis, portrays a greedy ape, Shift, who discovers a mysteriously forsaken lion skin and persuades a likable but gullible donkey, Puzzle, to wear it in the guise of being the true Aslan.[188] Puzzle is only presented as Aslan at night under the cloak of darkness with Shift as the sole spokesman. Whereas there are those who do not fall for the ruse, most do.

In spite of the evil signs in the heavens and the fact that no one has seen nor heard from Aslan in ages, most, even the well-intentioned, fall for the charade and are even told that Aslan is actually just another name for an evil and bloodthirsty deity worshipped by the Calormenes known as Tash. Likewise, the Scriptures foretell that at some point in the future here on earth, a global leader referred to as the antichrist will charade as Christ. I believe this charade will include the endorsement of fallen angels whom I believe may be disguised as extraterrestrials. Perhaps the antichrist may even appear to arrive in the clouds. However, the antichrist is just a donkey disguised in a lion skin. Let us not get "donkeyed" nor spiritually catfished in the ruse.

---

188 C. S. Lewis (Clive Staples), *The Last Battle* (Harper Collins Publishers, 2005) (first published September 4, 1956).

Celebrities affirming their belief in ETs is nothing new, but in recent times, many are starting to report their own personal close encounters and using social media to do so. Singer, actress, and activist Demi Lovato not only reported her encounter but posted the photos on Instagram in October 2020 to verify her story. Frankly, the video is unconvincing and underwhelming; the comments, however, were insightful. Many of those who responded to her post stated not only had they too seen a UFO, but some also expressed their hope for a new age of peace and unity that this advent would bring. Lovato said,

> Over the past couple of months I have dug deep into the science of consciousness and experienced not only peace and serenity like I've never known but I have also witnessed the most incredibly profound sightings in the sky as well as feet away from me. This planet is on a very negative path to destruction, but WE can change that together. If we were to get 1% of the population to mediate and make contact, we would force our government to acknowledge the truth about extraterrestrial life among us and change our destructive habits destroying our planet (...) to make contact yourself you can download the app and it

will teach you the protocols for connecting to life beyond our planet![189]

The popularity of UFOs is a direct reflection of a society that is spiritually hungry and looking for meaning and purpose in life that mistakenly believes will be fulfilled via contact with an extraterrestrial civilization. Their presupposition is that proof of life outside of planet Earth will provide meaning to life. *An overarching ingredient of the UFO phenomenon is that the search and hope for ETI is akin to a quest for an Extraterrestrial Savior.* Whether intentional or not, to some extent, components of History Channel's *Ancient Aliens* are promoting a type of religion or at least a spiritual worldview falsely teaching that extraterrestrials are our creator and that the hope of humanity lies in their return to save us.

It was the French mathematician Blaise Pascal who introduced the concept that humanity is created with a God-shaped vacuum, meaning that since we are created to be in relationship with God, we all sense that there's something missing until that void is filled. The writer of Ecclesiastes tells us that God has placed eternity in our hearts (Ecclesiastes 3:11). Many seek to fill this void through wealth, relationships, social justice causes, and

---

189 Paris Close, "Demi Lovato Claims She Contacted Aliens, Shares Shocking Footage," IHeart.com., 2020, https://www.iheart.com/content/2020-10-19-demi-lovato-claims-she-contacted-aliens-shares-shocking-footage/.

extraterrestrials—all of which are the equivalent of trying to fit a square peg into a round hole. Although they may serve as a "spiritual band-aid," sooner or later, the reality of their inadequacy sinks in.

In the Desert Southwest, we regularly go through droughts and months without rain or even a cloud in the sky. When a cloud does appear, there's some hope that maybe there will be rain, but more often than not, it fails to deliver what is anticipated. "Like clouds and wind without rain is one who boasts gifts never given" (Proverbs 25:14 NIV). Ezekiel describes false prophets as "jackals" (Ezekiel 13:4); they prey upon people's souls.

The sixth thing you should know about the UFO phenomenon is that it is rife with false prophets who are providing humanity with false hope.

Jesus alone provides the true answer as to why we're here and what our purpose is. There is most certainly an aspect of the UFO phenomenon that's being intentionally utilized to direct humanity away from Jesus and towards a false hope, but that's not all.

CHAPTER 7

Replication in His Image

So God created man in His own image. In the image of God, he created him; male and female he created them.

(Genesis 1:27 ESV)

If extraterrestrials are not biological beings, nor drones, A.I., or products from another terrestrial world, but rather fallen unholy angels, then what is their end game? In the same way that Christians are called to prepare the earth for Christ's return and rule, the devil is preparing the world for his rule and reign, including a battle he intends to win. You may be thinking, *Does he really think he can defeat God?*

Have you ever met a narcissist before? After showing Jesus the kingdoms of the world, Satan is brazen enough to say, "...All these I will give you, if you will fall down and worship me" (Matthew 4:9 ESV). The devil is the ultimate narcissist and believes that the world would be a better place if he were in charge, and he desires to be worshipped as a god. Perhaps he's hoping for a truce by showing God that most of humanity would rather follow him and thus cede control of the earth to his authority. Regardless, since he wants to be worshipped as a god, he seeks to change the grand narrative. Lucifer and those who follow him seek to portray him as a liberator and the rightful ruler of the world who falsely promises a better world under his rule rather than God's. If He wanted, God could've created a race of mindless robots, but instead, He provided the angels with a freedom of choice. Quite possibly, Lucifer was heaven's original worship leader but one day decided that rather than direct worship to God, he'd rather be worshipped himself. He was so charming, likable, and so convincing that other angelic beings also joined in. They were immediately cast out, but this hasn't discouraged Satan's objective.

Following a day of ministry, Christ's disciples shared what their day was like, including how they were able to cast out demons in Jesus' name. Jesus responded by letting them know that He was in heaven when Satan was cast out: "I saw Satan fall like lightning from heaven" (Luke 10:18 ESV). In Isaiah, the prophet is addressing the king of Babylon but then takes time to address the evil spirit behind the king—Satan—and says,

How you have fallen from heaven, morning star, son of the dawn! You have been cast
down to the earth, you who once laid low the
nations! You said in your heart, "I will ascend
to the heavens; I will raise my throne above
the stars of God; I will sit enthroned on the
mount of assembly, on the utmost heights of
Mount Zaphon. I will ascend above the tops
of the clouds; I will make myself like the Most
High."

(Isaiah 14:12–14 NIV)

More insight is provided when Ezekiel is propheti-
cally addressing the king of Tyre when the prophet
takes a moment to address the evil spirit behind Tyre's
king directly. Like Satan, the king of Tyre was prideful
and took all the credit for his position and power, and
had an insatiable appetite for more (Ezekiel 28:11–19).
Satan is a great imitator, and in an effort to be seen as a
creator, I believe he seeks to create his own race of soulless beings who are not in need of redemption through
Jesus and this may explain aspects of the abduction facet within the UFO phenomenon.

*The seventh thing you should know about the
UFO phenomenon is that evidence collected from*

**abduction encounters reveals that they have an
ungodly and evil fascination with human sexuality, which reveals their true colors.**

This perverted preoccupation has been around since
at least Genesis 6. Whenever you research or delve into
UFO phenomena, sooner or later, the Nephilim will
show up in the discussion.

> When man began to multiply on the face of
> the land and daughters were born to them,
> the sons of God saw that the daughters of
> man were attractive. And they took as their
> wives any they chose. Then the Lord said, "My
> Spirit shall not abide in man forever, for he is
> flesh: his days shall be 120 years." The Nephil-
> im were on the earth in those days, and also
> afterward, when the sons of God came in to
> the daughters of man and they bore children
> to them. These were the mighty men who
> were of old, the men of renown.
>
> (Genesis 6:1–4 ESV)

Many explanations and theories have been presented regarding the Nephilim (i.e., the "giants" or "fallen
ones" of Genesis 6; the Hebrew word Nephilim can be
translated as "the fallen ones" and is rooted in the word

"Nephal," which means "to be cast down," "fall away," or "to desert".[190]), but it's obvious at the very least that they were seeking to interfere with the procreation of humanity. Why? Three chapters before their appearance, we read, "And I will put enmity between you and the woman, and between your seed and her Seed; He shall bruise your head, and you shall bruise His heel" (Genesis 3:15 NKJV). This verse is referred to as the protoevangelium, i.e., "the first gospel". "The seed of the woman" is the first Messianic prophecy, a reference to Jesus. The Messiah would be born of a woman, ultimately the Virgin Mary, who would proceed to deal a death blow to the devil. It would be reasonable to infer that upon hearing this revelation, Satan would begin to take steps to oppose and prevent the fulfillment of this prophecy by destroying her offspring, i.e., seed.

Thus, presuming that Satan may have considered Abel as the referenced "seed," it's really no surprise that we see the first murder in the following chapter of Genesis (4:8). By Genesis 6, we see that not only is the entire earth corrupt and violent, but that something incredibly odd and perverse is taking place within human procreation.

---

190 John D. Barry ed., Lazarus Wentz ed., Douglas Mangum ed., Carrie Sinclair-Wolcott ed., Rachel Klippenstein ed., Elliot Ritzema ed., and Wendy Widder ed., "Nephilim." In *The Lexham Bible Dictionary* (Bellingham, WA: Lexham Press, 2016).

In my opinion, this interference was primarily an intentional attempt to prevent the Messiah, the "seed" of a human woman, from being born in the first place. By destroying and/or corrupting the genome of humans, there would be no genetically pure representation of humanity (cf. Romans 5:12, 19; 1 Corinthians 15:45–49) from which the Messiah was to be born. The perverse nature of the Nephilim compounds the rampant wickedness of the world, which was a catalyst for Noah's Flood.

"It's Alive! It's Alive!"

The 1931 film adaptation of Frankenstein by Mary Shelley depicts Dr. Victor Frankenstein's scientific efforts in using electricity to create life from the body parts of the deceased. After a successful experiment that brings the creature to life, he famously shouts, "It's alive! It's alive!"[191] Originally there was another line deleted from the final cut in which Dr. Frankenstein then said, "Now I know what it's like to be God."[192] However, since this was, at that time, considered blasphemy, this line was audio censored by a clap of thunder but restored to most editions in 1999. In some ways, this may depict Satan's aspirations as well. In regard to alien ab-

191 Wikipedia Contributors, "Frankenstein (1931 Film)," Wikipedia, The Free Encyclopedia, 2022, https://en.wikipedia.org/wiki/Frankenstein_(1931_film).

192 Ibid.

ductions, Dr. David Jacobs, who personally researched sixty abduction cases, said, "It is not a program of reproduction but one of production. They (aliens) are not here to help us; they have their own agenda."[193]

One aspect of the protoevangelium that's often overlooked is that it is preceded by the announcement that there will be "...enmity between you and the woman, and between *your* [the devil's] offspring and her [Eve's] offspring" (Genesis 3:15 ESV). "Sperm" is a Greek translation of the Hebrew word for "seed".[194] [195] The Septuagint, a Greek translation of the Hebrew Scriptures, i.e., the Old Testament, speaks of the "spermatos" of the woman and the "spermatos" of the serpent. Some versions will translate the Hebrew word for offspring as "seed."

Many abductees reveal an ongoing interest by the aliens in sexual reproduction. Dr. Derek Kidner, a British OT scholar and commentary author, said, "The craving of demons for a body, evident in the Gospels, offers at least some parallel to this hunger for a sexual experience."[196] Under the guise of being aliens from an-

---

193 David M. Jacobs, *Secret Life: Firsthand Accounts of UFO Abductions* (New York: Atria, 1992; Reprint edition (April 16, 1993).

194 Randall Tan and David A. deSilva, "Sperm," *The Lexham Greek-English Interlinear Septuagint: Rahlfs Edition* (Logos Bible Software, 2009), Ge 3:15.

195 Randall Tan ed. and David A. DeSilva ed., "Sperm," In *Dictionary of Biblical Languages w/ Semantic Domains: Hebrew (OT)* (Lexham Press, 2009.

196 Derek Kidner, *Genesis: An Introduction and Commentary*, Leicester: Inter-Varsity Press, 1967.

other world, the forces of darkness may be collecting and cataloging human DNA, and probably much more, for some nefarious project. In an interview with Bob Lazar by George Knapp of KLAS-TV in Las Vegas, Lazar claimed that there was a very high-level document regarding aliens and religion that was very thick in which humans were described as being "containers." When asked to elaborate (i.e., containers for what exactly?), he responded by saying, "That's supposedly how the aliens look at us; that we are nothing but containers. Maybe containers for souls. You can come up with whatever theory you want. But we're containers, and that's how we're mentioned in the documents."[197]

Jack Parsons, a successful rocket scientist with JPL (Jet Propulsion Laboratory), a known occultist (and friend of L. Ron Hubbard, the founder of Scientology), was hand-picked by none other than Luciferian Alister Crowley to lead the Agape Lodge in California, and regularly practiced rituals too profane to mention, but with the goal of creating a new breed of human. As bizarre as all of this may sound, a half-century of abduction accounts suggests that aliens are seeking to create their own version of humanity and/or perhaps biological bodies more conducive for demons to inhabit. Their interest in the human genome, in my opinion, suggests

---

197 Timothy Good, *Alien Liaison: The Ultimate Secret* (Arrow books, 1991); "Larry King Now: Season 7, Episode 72 - Rotten Tomatoes," 2019, https://www.rottentomatoes.com/tv/larry_king_now/s07/e72.

that they seek to produce some form of intelligent biological life. *The exact reasons are unknown, but in addition to wanting to be worshipped as God, throughout the ages, the devil has sought to mimic and imitate the One True God; I believe this includes the desire to create soulless life forms that will recognize him as their creator and who need not be redeemed by Jesus.*

Angelic Corporality?

The idea that something spiritual can affect the tangible is hard for us to get our heads around and explains why a number of alternative and even very plausible explanations have been put forth for Genesis 6:1–4. Whereas humanity was created with a physical body, soul, and spirit, the exact nature of the intelligent and pre-Adamic beings isn't revealed in Scripture and contains some ambiguity. Although angels are described as ministering spirits (Hebrews 1:14), we also know that some, if not all, can converse without the need for telepathy, drink, and eat. Whereas, it's probably being used metaphorically, "manna" is described as the "bread of angels" (Psalm 78:25).

Angels are able to execute the judgment of God, engage in battle, and have the vocal abilities to sing and deliver messages audibly. Fallen angels under the guise of ghosts, etc., sometimes leave scars on people's bodies, move objects, animals (i.e., the herd of pigs in Luke

8:32), and even people. In Mark's gospel, a bewildered father reports that the evil spirits in his son had often "*thrown* him into the fire or water to destroy him" (Mark 9:22 NET). Clearly, they can most certainly influence and manipulate the corporeal, apparently even being able to manufacture tangible items.

Elijah, who was discouraged and exhausted after running for his life from Jezebel, is awakened by an angel who had prepared him the modern-day equivalent of a pancake breakfast.

> He stretched out and fell asleep under the shrub. All of a sudden, an angelic messenger touched him and said, "Get up and eat." He looked and right there by his head was a cake baking on hot coals and a jug of water. He ate and drank and then slept some more. The Lord's angelic messenger came back again, touched him, and said, "Get up and eat, for otherwise you won't be able to make the journey."
>
> (1 Kings 19:5–7 NET)

In Revelation John said, "Then I saw an angel coming down from heaven, holding the *key* of the abyss and a great chain in his hand. And he laid hold of the dragon, the serpent of old, who is the devil and Satan, and

bound him for a thousand years" (Revelation 20:1–2).
Are the key and chain he witnessed allegorical or tangible? Both? Earlier in chapter thirteen of the same book,
very tangible actions are enforced by the false prophet.

And it was allowed to give breath to the image of the beast, so that the image of the beast
might even speak and might cause those who
would not worship the image of the beast to
be slain.

(Revelation 13:15 ESV)

At the very least, it's obvious that angels are capable
of manifesting themselves physically on earth within
limits (Genesis 18:8; 19:3). Angels themselves cannot reproduce. However, fallen angels can apparently engage
in what Chuck Missler described as "sexual mischief."
Their ability to appear human is so convincing that the
residents of Sodom sought to gang rape the angels that
showed up at Lot's home. This ability to take on the
form of a human even serves as the basis of an exhor-
tation from the author of Hebrews reminding us to be
kind to strangers (Hebrews 13:2). Angels have what we
could refer to in contemporary vernacular as superpow-
ers. "...They kept bringing pressure on Lot and moved
forward to break down the door. But the angels inside
reached out and *pulled Lot* back into the house and shut

the door. Then they *struck the men* who were at the door of the house, young and old, *with blindness*. (Genesis 19:9–11 emphasis mine). It's reasonable to presume that the angels who followed Lucifer's rebellion retained many if not all of their capabilities.

In Ephesians 6:12 (ESV), the Bible says, "For we do not wrestle against flesh and blood, but against the rulers, against the authorities, against the cosmic powers of this present darkness, against the spiritual forces of evil in the heavenly places." This is insightful in revealing a very real spiritual realm of non-human intelligent beings that regularly interact and interface with humanity. The first biblical description of the devil indicates that he's "crafty" (Genesis 3:1), and we can presume the same can be said of fallen angels. Although dominion of the earth has been granted by God to humanity (a plan that has been interrupted and opposed, but not abandoned), it may be a little hard on the human ego to acknowledge that the events of the universe are not completely centered upon us. In the grand cosmic scheme of things, as far as intelligent beings go, we're the newcomers and even described as being a little lower than the angels (Psalm 8:5).

In addition to this, Revelation 13 indicates that the False Prophet will have the ability to perform *miracles*. "It performs great signs, even making fire come down from heaven to earth in front of people" (Revelation 13:13

ESV). This demonstrates that the forces of darkness have the capability to perform great feats of wonder. I propose that this could include the ability to appear as a being or a spacecraft from another world. The Bible reveals that angels can likewise appear and disappear. "(UFOs) behave as if they're alive. It seemed as if they could read my mind. I don't think they're mechanical at all. I got the distinct impression that it was alive."[198] Angels, holy and fallen, are intelligent, spiritual beings who are not limited to all of earth's natural laws—they're inter-dimensional. In Acts 12:6–17, we're given a glimpse into some of the capabilities and powers that angels possess. In this particular scene, Peter has been arrested and is awaiting a trial. However, Luke tells us that an angel is sent to break him out of jail. This jailbreak includes the removal of physical objects like shackles and the opening of prison gates while everyone else is asleep. Somewhat like a holy abduction encounter, Peter is initially unable to discern if he's asleep or awake. In this case, an apostle is freed by an angel to continue in his ministry of proclaiming the gospel. We can deduce that fallen angels may also use these same powers and capabilities for nefarious purposes.

For most Bible scholars and commentators, Genesis 6:1–4 is a troubling account. Read at face value, beings

---

198 John A. Keel, *Operation Trojan Horse: The Classic Breakthrough Study of UFOs* (New York: Anomalist Books, 2007), 44.

described as "sons of God" (Hebrew: "B'nai ha Elohim") are sexually attracted to the "daughters of men" (i.e., daughters of Adam, aka "benoth Adam") who, upon copulating, produced offspring referred to as Nephilim, aka "mighty men" and "men of renown." A snippet of the backstory is provided in Jude.

> You also know that the angels who did not keep within their proper domain, but abandoned their own place of residence, He has kept in eternal chains in utter darkness, locked up for the judgment of the Great Day. So also Sodom and Gomorrah and the neighboring towns, since they indulged in sexual immorality and pursued unnatural desire in a similar way to these angels, are now displayed as an example by suffering the punishment of eternal fire.
>
> (Jude 1:6–7, NET)

This indicates that these angelic beings proactively sought to "fornicate" with the daughters of men and that they went after "strange flesh," which means flesh of a different kind from theirs. Not only did these angelic beings classified as "sons of God" leave heaven to engage in this perversity, but based upon Jude's use of the aorist tense of "apolipontas" this was a decision for which there was no road back.

Obviously, the idea that fallen angels (i.e., fallen "sons of God") could look with lust upon, much less reproduce with human women, is incompatible with our understanding of spiritual beings. However, this perception is quite likely more influenced by the Age of Reason rather than the Bible itself. The idea that the Nephilim were the offspring of fallen angels and human females was not only represented in the beliefs of the early church (and Judaism, for that matter), but it is quite likely the impetus behind Egyptian, Greek, and Roman mythologies that represent a similar narrative. In an effort to be like God, Satan seeks to be a pseudo-father by creating life. He also wants and needs more followers who need him, not God.

It was the understanding of the first-century Church that it would be in the best interest of women to take steps to avoid the unwanted attraction of supernatural beings. The Church at Corinth was without biblical roots, and so in his first letter to them regarding some of the basics of church life, Paul writes, "For this reason, and *because the angels are watching*, a woman should wear a covering on her head to show she is under authority" (1 Corinthians 11:10 NLT, emphasis mine). Granted, this is descriptive rather than prescriptive, but nonetheless, it reveals the mindset of the first-century Church.

In case you're thinking to yourself, *well, that's the NLT. It's not a concordant translation*; the ESV, NASB, KJV, NKJV, and NIV likewise use the phrase "because of the

angels." 1 Peter 3:19, 2 Peter 2:4, Jude 1:6–7, and the apoc-
ryphal Book of Enoch allude to the imprisonment of the
fallen "sons of God" (a group of fallen angels) that in-
stigated and participated in this nefarious project (that
produced the Nephilim) have already been cast into the
abyss, the same place Satan will eventually be incarcer-
ated for a thousand years (Revelation 20:2).

Church Fathers and Ancient Christian Writings

This view that fallen angels interfered with and perverted humanity's procreation is reflected in the earliest, non-biblical Christian writings, such as the Books
of 1 Enoch (6:2ff) and Jubilees (5:1) as well as the writings of the Essenes found in the Dead Sea Scrolls (1 Qap;
Genesis 2:1; CD 2:17–19). The earliest Christian writers
(e.g., Justin, Irenaeus, Clement of Alexandria, Tertullian, Origen) also reflect this presumption and it was
alluded to in the more ancient historical writings of Jo-
sephus and Philo.[199] Irenaeus (130–202 AD), a disciple of
Polycarp and the bishop of the church in Lyons, France,
wrote:

> And for a very long while wickedness extended
> and spread, and reached and laid hold upon
> the whole race of mankind, until a very small

---

199 Charles Duke Yonge (Translator), *The Works of Philo: Complete and Unabridged* (Hendrickson Pub, 1993), 152.

seed of righteousness remained among them and illicit unions took place upon the earth, since angels were united with the daughters of the race of mankind; and they bore to them sons who for their exceeding greatness were called giants.[200]

Justin Martyr (100–165 AD) said, "...the angels transgressed this appointment and were captivated by the love of women."[201] Tertullian (155–220 AD) wrote:

We are instructed, moreover, by our sacred book how from certain angels who fell of their own free-will, there sprang a more wicked demon-brood, condemned of God along with the authors of their race, and that chief we have referred to. It will for the present be enough, however, that some account is given of their work. Their great business in the ruin of mankind. So, from the very first, spiritual wickedness sought our destruction. They in-

200 Irenaeus, Saint, Bishop of Lyon, The Demonstration of the Apostolic Preaching, Translated from the Armenian with Introduction and Notes by J. Armitage Robinson - Internet Archive, Open Library (London: S.P.C.K., 1920), 18, http://link.archive.org/portal/The-demonstration-of-the-Apostolic-preaching/l357e9BHcCA/.

201 Justin Martyr, "The Second Apology of Justin," Justin Martyr, Second Apology, Accessed April 29, 2022, Chapter V, https://www.biblestudytools.com/history/early-church-fathers/ante-nicene/vol-1-apostolic-with-justin-martyr-irenaeus/justin-martyr/second-apology-of-justin.html.

flict, accordingly, upon our bodies diseases and other grievous calamities, while by violent assaults they hurry the soul into sudden and extraordinary excesses.[202]

This view that fallen angels intervened to disrupt and interfere with the human genome is also reflected in the writings of Clement of Rome (35–99AD) and Lactantius (250–325AD).[203] Although God intervened to disrupt this plan, including a global flood, it demonstrates their ability to interfere and influence humanity physically on a grand scale.

This modus operandi is one that, in my opinion, has been retooled for different purposes—to create life. As Dr. John Mack said, "We simply do not know what to do with a phenomenon that crossed that seemingly inviolable barrier. It shocks the foundation of our belief structure, our minds have no place to put such a thing."[204] Without a doubt, this is a challenging concept to get our brain

202 Tertullian, *Tertullian: The Apology, Translated by Wm. Reeve* (Griffith, Farran, Okeden & Welsh Newberry House, 1709 Reprinted 1889), Chapter XXII, https://www.tertullian.org/articles/reeve_apology.htm.

203 Clement I, Pope, "The Clementine Homilies: Clement I, Pope: Free Download, Borrow, and Streaming: Internet Archive," In The Clementine Homilies (Edinburgh T. & T. Clark, 1870), Chapter XIII, https://archive.org/details/clementinehomili00clem; "CHURCH FATHERS: Divine Institutes, Book II (Lactantius)," New Advent, Accessed April 29, 2022, Chapter XV, https://www.newadvent.org/fathers/07015.htm.

204 John Mack, *Abduction: Human Encounters with Aliens* (Scribner, 2007), 146.

around, but as the fictional character Hamlet said, "There are more things in heaven and earth, Horatio, than are dreamt of in your philosophy."[205]

205 William Shakespeare, "Hamlet Act 1 Scene 5," Genius, Accessed April 29, 2022. https://genius.com/William-shakespeare-hamlet-act-1-scene-5-annotated.

CHAPTER 8

A Cosmic Reset and Concentration Camp

When the moon is in the Seventh House. And
Jupiter aligns with Mars. Then peace will
guide the planets. And love will steer the stars.
This is the dawning of the age of Aquarius.
—*Aquarius/Let the Sun Shine In*
by The Fifth Dimension

The term "Great Reset" is not a biblical term. Rather,
it's used to describe the concept, some would say the
agenda, for a better world. You can find the endorsement of the ideology on the World Economic Forum's
(WEF) website. Regardless of whether or not the WEF
achieves its goal, elements of this ideology have appeared in the past, and humanity will most certainly see
some of the aspects it proposes before Christ's return.

I believe that the UFO phenomena may play a "behind the scenes" role in this reset, but my theory will

require some background information. So, please stay with me and let me explain the Great Reset by first explaining a micro-reset.

The 20th century provides at least two examples of micro-resets; the *New Deal* and the *Marshall Plan*. There are a number of factors that led up to the infamous 1929 stock market crash. However, there's a general consensus that the primary factors were overconfidence in the economy and high inflation rates, which subsequently contributed to a panic resulting in hordes of people rushing to withdraw cash from their banks.

Remember how everyone was stocking up on toilet paper in late Spring 2020? The same thing happened in 1929, except with cash. This is somewhat illustrated in the "bank run" scene of the Christmas classic, *It's a Wonderful Life*. In addition to the general public, investors were unable to withdraw their money because bank officials had invested the money into the market—a market that had subsequently crashed. Four years later, FDR introduced the *New Deal*, which included a monetary reform in which the U.S. Dollar was moved off the gold standard and mandated Americans to exchange their gold for currency at a fixed rate; failure to do so resulted in fines and incarceration.

Another example would be the *Marshall Plan*. Following World War II, an initiative led by the U.S. rebuilt Germany with a new government, currency, laws, and borders; Germany was reset. These are just two 20th-century examples of micro-resets. The point is that a crisis of great magnitude is needed for a national micro-reset. A global reset would most likely require a crisis of global proportions making the idea not only more palatable but practical.

The aspiration of the WEF for a *Great Reset* is that it be all-encompassing for every nation on the planet. The proposal for the WEF's Great Reset can be found on their website.[206] So, just to be clear, *it's not a conspiracy theory.* The WEF is not a governmental organization with the power to implement or enforce its ideals, but they are very influential, and they work with governments all over the world regarding finances. On their website, they describe the core components as the following:

1. Recreate society into a stakeholder economy.
2. Build a more resilient way of government for the world.
3. Harness the innovations and developments of the fourth industrial revolution (Artificial Intelligence, Transhumanism, Bio-technologies, etc.) for the good of humanity.[207]

Their goal is to shape and "reset" national agendas into one global agenda. This "Great Reset" will require

---

206 "The Great Reset," World Economic Forum, 2022, https://www.weforum.org/great-reset.

207 "The Great Reset," 2022.

the deconstruction of the existing national agendas and push the "reset" button for a global agenda. The curricula of many public schools and most state universities promote its core components, and there seems to be an understanding among many global leaders that the world needs to be reset. Prince Charles said, "I hope you will join me to drive a new Marshall-like plan for nature, people; and the planet. We need a shift in our economic model that places nature and the world's transition to net-zero at the heart of how we operate, prioritizing the pursuit of sustainable inclusive growth in the decades to come."[208]

On a 2020 episode of The Today Show, Al Gore said, "This is the time for a Great Reset."[209] John Kerry said, "This is a big moment. The World Economic Forum (...) is really going to have to play a front and center role in refining the Great Reset to deal with climate change and inequity—all of which is being laid bare as a consequence of COVID-19."[210] Justin Trudeau said,

208 "Prince Charles Says We Need a Global Marshall Plan to Save the Environment," World Economic Forum, 2020, https://www.weforum.org/videos/prince-charles-says-we-need-a-global-marshall-plan-to-save-the-environment.

209 Al Gore Talks Climate Crisis: 'This Is the Time for a Great Reset,'" 2020, NBC News Universal: Today Show, https://www.today.com/video/al-gore-talks-climate-crisis-this-is-the-time-for-a-great-reset-85439045592.

210 Justin Haskins, "John Kerry Reveals Biden's Devotion to Radical 'Great Reset' Movement," The Hill, 2020, https://thehill.com/opinion/energy-environment/528482-john-kerry-reveals-bidens-devotion-to-radical-great-reset-movement/.

"Canada believes that a strong, coordinated response across the world and across sectors is essential. This pandemic has provided an opportunity for a reset."[211]

I could go on, but from the proverbial horse's mouth, Klaus Schwab, the Executive Chairman of the WEF, said, "The COVID-19 crisis has shown us that our old systems are not fit anymore for the 21st century. In short, we need a Great Reset."[212] Another way of looking at the proposed "Great Reset" could be described as global socialism and communism, including the control of advanced technology.

The two primary monkey wrenches to these ideals are sovereign nation states and prosperity. Desperate times call for desperate measures is a well-known idiom that contains elements of truth. Nations that voluntarily become communist generally do so out of desperation, i.e., there's no other solution. In exchange for complete allegiance and loss of private property, a communist leader offers hope, a game plan, and practical amenities (i.e., food and water). Citizens are promised

---

211 "Global News: Coronavirus: Trudeau Tells UN Conference That Pandemic Provided 'Opportunity for a Reset,'" 2020, YouTube. 2020, https://www.youtube.com/watch?v=n2fp0Jeyjvw; Media, Sun, "EDITORIAL: Trudeau Sees Pandemic as an 'Opportunity,'" Toronto Sun, 2020, https://torontosun.com/opinion/editorials/editorial-trudeau-sees-pandemic-as-an-opportunity.

212 Klaus Schwab, "Now Is the Time for a 'great Reset' of Capitalism," World Economic Forum, 2020, https://www.weforum.org/agenda/2020/06/now-is-the-time-for-a-great-reset/.

a roof over their heads, but in exchange for the loss of private property.

Imagine the desperation that would be created by a pandemic with just a slightly higher, say 5%, mortality rate than COVID-19 or even a natural disaster on a nationwide scale (e.g., a super volcano in Yellowstone, an asteroid hit, a drought worse than the nationwide dust bowl of 1930s America). What would happen if there was a war in which the U.S. had a stalemate or worse, or a financial collapse like the stock market crash of 1929? Any of these scenarios on a grand scale could all result in the conditions of a reset for any nation being more palatable, even for the U.S. I believe that an international disclosure of contact with ETs may also be used to fuel the fires of a Great Reset.

In a CNN podcast interview, President Barak Obama stated that if UFOs are aliens, he hopes that they would serve as a catalyst for humanity to find common ground.[213] What if the United Nations announced that they had made contact with an ETC? In a 1982 address to the United Nations, America's 40th president, Ronald Reagan, said, "Perhaps we need some outside, universal threat to make us recognize this common bond. I occasionally think how quickly our differences worldwide

213 Ezra Klein, "Opinion | Barack Obama Interview: Joe Biden Is 'Finishing the Job,'" The New York Times, 2021, https://www.nytimes.com/2021/06/01/opinion/ezra-klein-podcast-barack-obama.html.

would vanish if we were facing an alien threat from outside this world."[214]

General Douglas MacArthur, America's last five-star general who led U.S. forces in WWI, WWII, and Korea, is often misquoted on the topic. Still, he did indeed allude to the concept of war with extraterrestrials in statements that referenced an "ultimate conflict between a united human race and the sinister forces of some other planetary galaxy."[215] An announcement that contact had been made with an ETC, even a staged one, could create or compound a crisis that would make the world more open to a great reset, including a religious one that could be leveraged for establishing a global interfaith community. Author Brad Steiger said, "Contactees have been told that the Space Beings hope to guide Earth to a period of great unification (...) (they) also seek to bring about a single, solidified government, which will conduct itself on spiritual principles and permit all of its citizens to grow constructively in love."[216]

In John's vision of the future, we're told that Jesus will return with the clouds (Revelation 1:7). Given his

214 Ronald Reagan, "Address by President Ronald Reagan to the UN General Assembly," U.S. Department of State, 1986, https://2009-2017.state.gov/p/io/potusunga/207357.htm.

215 "'Duty, Honor, Country' by General Douglas MacArthur, May 12, 1962," The Art of Manliness, 2022, https://www.artofmanliness.com/duty-honor-country-by-general-douglas-macarthur/.

216 Brad Steiger, *The Fellowship: Spiritual Contact between Humans and Outer Space Beings* (Doubleday, 1988), 51.

track record in perverting all that God does, it shouldn't come as a surprise if the devil creates his version of a second coming by appearing to return in the clouds as earth's savior and liberator.

The two most popular reasons given by Ufologists for the U.S. Government's concealment of ETI are that it would disrupt the economy and shatter the Judeo-Christian belief system that provides a type of moral glue to society. Indeed, if a spaceship landed on the lawn of the White House in broad daylight and with complete coverage by all the major networks, it would bring the world to a stop... for a while. With the advent of continuous and global news coverage, many of us can still recall how the national tragedy of September 11, 2001, briefly affected our nation. A disclosure of contact with an ETC would most certainly spread around the world in minutes, necessitating a "where do we go from here?" and "who's our spokesperson?" moment.

According to an updated December 31, 2020, Bloomberg article, approximately 340 U.S. companies, including airlines, restaurants, oil producers, gyms, and restaurants that went out of business in the past fiscal year did so as a result of COVID-19.[217] Thus, if the government did indeed have proof of ET life, there very well

---

217 Davide Scigliuzzo, Josh Saul, Shannon D. Harrington, Claire Boston, and Demetrios Pogkas, "Bankrupt Companies 2020: Businesses That Went Bust Because of Covid, Guitar Center to Francesca's," Bloomberg L.P., 2020, https://www.bloomberg.com/graphics/2020-us-bankruptcies-coronavirus/.

may be some cause for economic concern in releasing such information. However, one piece of vital information conveniently neglected in this conspiracy theory is that a significant percentage of UFO sightings take place *outside* of the U.S. and in nations that do not have the best interests of the U.S., Western civilization, or Christianity in mind. Russia and China, for example, are also investigating UFO phenomena, and it can be assured that if they are in possession of sufficient evidence that they feel would discredit Christianity, bankrupt the U.S., and position them as the global leader for interacting with an ETC they would most certainly present the evidence.

Therefore, it may be an issue of timing. The devil is an opportunist, and it's reasonable to presume that he may be planning to use UFOs as an additional or supplemental reason for creating buy-in for his aspirations for a global government for which he is the leader. At some point, our planet will experience a global crisis, and the governments of the world will collectively be looking for answers and a leader.

The eighth thing you should know about UFOs, real or imagined, is that they may be used for supplementing the creation of a global ecumenical religion.

An Explanation for the Rapture?

Regardless of whether you believe in a pre, mid, or post-tribulation rapture of the Church, could it be that the devil is also uncertain of its timing and, in an effort to cover his bases for missing people, is seeking to condition the world to view it not as a rapture but rather as a mass alien abduction?

Whereas Christ's return to rule and reign on the earth (Second Coming) is an element of essential Christian doctrine, the term rapture is used to refer to the belief in an event in which Christians will be "caught up" in the air (evacuated) in the last days. Those who refer to themselves as "Pre-Tribulationists" believe that this event will take place immediately prior to the Great Tribulation (cf. Revelation 6–19). "Mid-Tribulationists" believe that the Rapture will occur halfway through the Great Tribulation, and "Post-Tribulationists" believe that it will occur at the conclusion of the Great Tribulation.

> Then we who are alive, who are left, will be caught up together with them in the clouds, to meet the Lord in the air, and so we will always be with the Lord.
>
> (1 Thessalonians 4:17 ESV; cf. Matthew 24:40–42, 1 Corinthians 15:50–52)

I have some very well-meaning, well-researched, and good-natured friends who all believe in Christ's return, but each can also make a very good case for their position (pre, mid, or post) on the Rapture. Could it be that the devil isn't completely certain either but wants to have an answer for the missing people should it be pre or mid? I think yes.

Some New Agers teach that all that's needed for a new age, an Age of Aquarius, in which the world would experience peace and harmony, is the adaptation of pluralism. "For New Agers, this will mean the end of the Christian era and the beginning of a new age symbolized by Aquarius, the water bearer, pouring water over the earth to heal the planet and cause mankind's problems to disappear, 'submerged into a great cosmic consciousness.'"[218] Some New Age adherents believe that the Age of Aquarius began on March 20, 2021. Regardless, due to the fact that Christians believe in salvation exclusively through Jesus, New Agers perceive Christianity as a hurdle (I prefer firewall) to global pluralism (i.e., universal ecumenicalism).

Perhaps it would be explained by the Antichrist's system that the Christians have been taken away to be re-educated and conditioned, i.e., in a cosmic concentration camp, but will return once their worldview has

---

218 Fritz Ridenour and Robert Williams, *So What's the Difference?: A Look at the 20 Worldviews, Faiths and Religions and How They Compare to Christianity* (Ventura, CA: Bethany House, 2001), 150.

been adjusted. Or, like everything else, perhaps the devil wants to mimic the idea of a rapture by creating his version of it.

In *Bringers of the Dawn*, New Age author, Barbara Marciniak, says, "The people who leave the planet during the time of Earth changes do not fit in here any longer, and they are stopping the harmony of Earth. When the time comes that perhaps 20 million people leave the planet at one time there will be a tremendous shift in consciousness for those who are remaining."[219] Other New Age writers refer to a "Great Exodus"[220] or "Great Evacuation" and, in some cases, even use the verbiage "in the twinkling of an eye" for referencing a mass abduction.

The ninth thing you should know about the UFO phenomenon is that it may be used as a way of explaining the Rapture.

I would venture to say that as a contingency plan, the devil has a prepared statement and response for either a pre- or mid-tribulation rapture and that such an event could be explained by or blamed on ETs. In addition to

219 Barbara Marciniak and Tera Thomas *Bringers of the Dawn: Teachings from the Pleiadians* (Bear & Co., 1992).

220 Timothy Green Tuella, *Project World Evacuation: UFOs to Assist in the "Great Exodus" of Human Souls off This Planet* (Inner Light Publications, 1993), 119.

the chaos an event such as the Rapture would cause, the world would be looking for an answer as to where their loved ones, co-workers, and friends had gone. Perhaps the disappearance of Christians could be explained as somewhat of a cosmic field trip for the purpose of re-educating their worldview for being a part of the intergalactic community needed for living in a new age of global pluralism. Actually, and somewhat ironically, Christians will indeed return, but to rule and reign on earth with Jesus Christ, the true and only Prince of Peace.

> Then the kingdom and dominion, and the greatness of the kingdoms under the whole heaven, shall be given to the people, the saints of the Most-High. His kingdom is an everlasting kingdom, and all dominions shall serve and obey Him.
>
> (Daniel 7:27 ESV; cf. Timothy 2:12; Revelation 5:10, 20:4–6)

Travis Walton and Bobby Brewer in Heber, Arizona

After missing for five days, Walton made a collect phone call from this phone booth. Walton said that he made the first call from the booth on the far right, but it was out of order before using the one in the middle.

Bobby Brewer and Travis Walton

*It was off of this logging road that Walton saw a UFO
at the tree line and was subsequently abducted.*

Nick Pope and Bobby Brewer

*Pope is a frequent contributor to History Channel's "Ancient Aliens".
In an effort to broaden the UFO phenomenon beyond tangible objects,
he was the first to introduce the term UAP (Unidentified Aerial
Phenomenon), meaning that it may or may not be a physical object.*

Lockheed F-94 Starfire

In 1952, F-94s were scrambled to intercept UFOs over Washington D.C.

SR-71

Also known as the "Blackbird," Lockheed's SR-71 was the U2's successor that flew higher and faster.

F-22 Raptor

Introduced in 2005, the Lockheed Martin F-22 employs stealth technology.

P-59 Bell Airacomet

In 1942 Bell aircraft was secretly developing and testing a jet
fighter, the P-59 Airacomet. It was so secret that they even
mounted a wooden propeller to the front of it while in the
hangar. Jack Woolams, in addition to being a great pilot, was
also somewhat of a practical joker who would fly into forma-
tions of P-51 mustangs and get just close enough for them to
see him wearing a gorilla mask. The fact that it flew without
a propeller by a "non-human" at "unfathomable speeds"
resulted in UFO reports from military pilots.

Phoenix Lights

A series of UFOs that were observed by thousands
of Phoenix residents on March 13, 1997.

CHAPTER 9

Astro-Apologetics

Today, rock 84001 speaks to us across all those billions of years and millions of miles. It speaks of the possibilities of life. If this discovery is confirmed [it wasn't], it will surely be one of the most stunning insights into our universe that science has ever uncovered. Its implications are as far-reaching and awe-inspiring as can be imagined.

—Bill Clinton, 1996

President Bill Clinton's premature and erroneous announcement that evidence for life on Mars had been found in a meteorite known as AL84001 reveals the desperation and hope for something more meaningful in life. The great psychoanalyst Carl Jung, for example, pointed out that the theme of humanity's rescue by extraterrestrial beings is a myth recast in technological guise: modern people who are no longer able to believe that humankind will be saved by God can believe that we will be saved by powerful godlike beings from other worlds. In an expression that succinctly captures this general interpretative approach to UFOs, Jung referred to flying saucers as "technological angels."[221]

Jung suggested that people who'd given up hope in humanity being saved or rescued by God would begin to look for other saviors such as technology or "god-like beings from other worlds."[222] In an interview with the *New York Times*, Barak Obama stated that an affirmation of ET life would result in new religions popping up and that would fundamentally change global society,[223] reflecting a prevalent misnomer that confirmation of ET life would make Christianity obsolete. Astronomer and Planetary Physicist Robert Jastrow says, "when we make contact with them, it will be a transforming event. I do not know how the Judeo-Christian tradition will react to this development because it will be hard to fit in, the concept that beings superior to us exist, not only technically, but perhaps spiritually and morally."[224]

Other "celebrity" astronomers and scientists suggest that it would be "back to the drawing board: for all the

221 James R. Lewis, *The Gods Have Landed: New Religions from Other Worlds* (State University of New York Press, 1995), xiii.

222 Ibid.

223 Klein, 2021.

224 Fred Heeren, *Show Me God: What the Message from Space Is Telling Us About God, Vol. 1* (Wheeling, IL: Day Star Publications, 2004).

major religions once ET life is confirmed." Astronomer and planetary physicist Robert Jastrow said,

> When we make contact with them (ETs), it will be a transforming event. I do not know how the Judeo-Christian tradition will react to this development, because the concept that there exist beings superior to us in this universe, not only technically, but perhaps spiritually and morally, will take some rethinking, I think, of the classic doctrines of Western religion. Whether aliens will deliver a knockout blow to any particular religion depends, of course, upon exactly what aliens have to tell us about God. Materialists have traditionally assumed that Jews, Christians, and Muslims, believing in a transcendent God, will receive bad news. And the Christian belief in Jesus' death for human sin seems particularly problematic to them. How could we reconcile Jesus' death for all with the existence of other intelligent creatures in the universe?[225]

I disagree. Here's why:

---

225 Fred Heeren, "Home Alone in the Universe?" First Things, 2002, https://www.firstthings.com/article/2002/03/home-alone-in-the-universe-36.

The tenth thing you should know about UFOs is that if aliens do exist, God is their Creator too.

The opening statement of the Bible says, "In the beginning, God created the heavens and the earth" (Genesis 1:1 NKJV). John tells us that "All things came into being through Him, and apart from Him not even one thing came into being that has come into being" (John 1:3 NASB). Therefore, such a discovery would not nullify Christian doctrine but rather confirm the extent of God's creative capabilities. We're naturally prone to think that everything in the universe revolves around us, but regarding the creation of intelligent beings, humans are the new kids on the block.

The Book of Job is somewhat of a cosmic opera in which the bottom of Job's life has completely dropped out and fallen apart, resulting in the obvious question; why does God allow bad things to happen to good people (i.e., theodicy)? After thirty chapters of Job's "friends" theorizing why bad things happen to good people, God Himself begins to ask some questions, one of which is: "Where were you when (...) the morning stars sang together, and all the *sons of God* shouted for joy?" at earth's creation (Job 38:4–7 ESV). "Sons of God" and "morning stars" are references to pre-Adamic intelligent and emotive angelic beings.

These particular beings referenced in Job are older than the earth itself. Perhaps the writings of J.R.R. Tolkien were influenced by this concept in his portrayal of the "Eldar" (Elves who are described as being the first intelligent children of Iluvatar) race in *The Silmarillion*. It is very clear from Scripture and creation that God delights in being creative. For example, when God created the angels, He didn't create just one type, but rather cherubim and seraphim, just to name a few.

The "spirits in prison" and the "four living creatures" also serve as examples of the variety of different intelligent life forms described in the Bible that were in existence before humanity (1 Peter 3:19; Ezekiel 1:5, 8–10, 12; Revelation 4:8, 5:8, 6:6, 14:3, 15:7, 19:4). Therefore, it shouldn't really come as a huge surprise to Christians if there are other intelligent life forms in the universe of which we simply have no biblical record.

Hebrews 11:3 says, "by faith we understand that the worlds were prepared by the Word of God..." (NASB). Could some of these "worlds" be places like our world, earth, where intelligent and emotive beings that God has created dwell? Whereas everything was created just right on earth for humanity and the animal kingdom, the universe itself was not created exclusively for humanity but for God's purposes.

Earthlings in His Image

The Bible does not provide exhaustive knowledge regarding the creation of the universe. Nevertheless, the revelation that we are given is insightful on the subject of ETI because we are told that God created humanity—earthlings—in His image (Genesis 1:26a, 27). Although we are given a broad spectrum of what God created, only humanity is given the exclusive designation of being created in the "image of God". Whereas we are informed that God created other cosmic bodies outside of our solar system, we are not told about any other creatures that were also created in the image of God.

Of course, an absence of a biblical reference to ETI does not necessitate a state of non-existence, nor can a dogmatic belief in ETI be positively affirmed from Scripture, but we are told that earthlings have been created in God's image and that He desires to be in relationship with each of us for all eternity.

The Bible was never intended to address every topic, but it does address the most important topic—*humanity's need for redemption*. When Jesus commissioned the disciples to spread the Good News (Matthew 28:18–20; Acts 1:8), He directed them to spread the good news that redemption is available through Him to the "uttermost parts of the *earth*" (emphasis mine). Whereas we have no special revelation demonstrating God's interest in people groups outside of Earth, you don't have to read between the lines to understand that God has a great interest in the people of planet Earth.

Even if humans can one day colonize the moon and Mars, the humans who reside there will likewise need redemption; wherever earthlings go, the sin virus will follow. Likewise, wherever humans go, God's great love will follow (cf. Psalm 139). God seeks to be in a relationship with every human and came in person (Jesus) to provide that opportunity for everyone. Of Jesus, the Bible says, "He is the radiance of the glory of God and the exact imprint of his nature, and he upholds the universe by the word of his power" (Hebrews 1:3 ESV). In the same chapter (vs. 10), the readers are reminded that the heavens are the work of His hands.

The bottom line for humanity is the fact that, regardless of the existence of ETI, we on earth are spiritually corrupt (Romans 3:13, 23; 6:23) and in need of a Savior for forgiveness and everlasting life, which is only available through Jesus (cf. John 3:16; Acts 4:12).

The eleventh thing you should know about the UFO phenomenon is that earthlings need Jesus.

If a global disclosure of ET life were affirmed and revealed tomorrow, you'd still have bills to pay. You and your spouse would still have disagreements, and people would still be influenced by drugs and addictions. People would still lie, cheat, steal, and kill. Humanity would still be separated from God. Earthlings would still be mortal and experience death and attend funerals. The necessity of being reconciled to God is still derived exclusively from the death, burial, and bodily resurrection of Jesus Christ.

Unlike any other creature, humanity was created in the image of God (Genesis 1:26), and God Himself has initiated reconciliation with us by taking on the form of a human and paying the price for our sin. Therefore, because only God can provide a solution to the root of humanity's core problem—sin, the presupposition that the discovery of ETI would fill this vacuum and reconcile us to God is erroneous and misleading. Jesus, being a son of Adam, and the Creator of the earth itself, is the sole rightful ruler. Because of His amazing grace, God has offered redemption to us and even the opportunity to rule and reign with Him.

There's Something Special about Earth

The more we learn about the universe, the more we understand how unique Earth and our solar system actually are. In fact, the scientific evidence not only points to the intelligent design but the uniqueness of the earth. Consider the following:

- Distance from sun: Earth just happens to be the right distance from the sun; if the earth were a little closer to the sun, the temperatures would be too extreme to sustain life, and if much further, global temperatures would be too frigid.

- Earth's tilt: The earth's tilt on its axis provides just the right inclination to prevent temperature extremes.

- Earth's rotation: If the Earth's rotation were more rapid, the wind speeds would be too great. If much slower, we'd regularly bake and freeze.

- Earth's moon: Our moon is just the right size; if it were much larger, there would be massive tidal flooding, and if much smaller, the oceans would stagnate.

- Ozone layer: Earth has an ozone layer to protect life from solar radiation.

- Oxygen: At 21%, Earth has just the right percentage of oxygen. A much richer mix would potentially provide too flammable of an environment, whereas if the availability were too little, humanity would not be able to exist.

- Jupiter: Our solar system has a planet of the right size and distance that serves as a comet sweeper, helping to protect the Earth from catastrophic asteroids.

- Safe Zone: In addition to being located in a safer part of the Milky Way, in between the spiral arms of Sagittarius and Perseus, we are also located safely distant from the nucleus of the galaxy.[226]

In *The Case for a Creator*, Lee Strobel reports the following analysis from Dr. Guillermo Gonzalez:

> In terms of habitability, I think we are in the best possible place. That's because our location provides enough building blocks to yield an Earth, while providing a low level of threats to life. I really can't come up with an example of another place in the galaxy that is as friendly to life as our location. Sometimes people claim you can be in any part of the galaxy, well, I've studied other regions—spiral arms, galactic centers, globular clusters, edge of disks—and no matter where it is, it's worse for life. I can't think of any better place than where we are.[227]

As Fred Heeren says, "Apparently our solar system is the freakish one."[228] Likewise, geologist Peter Ward and

---

226 Elizabeta Maksimovska, "What If Earth Was Near the Center of the Milky Way?" INSH World, 2019, https://insh.world/science/what-if-earth-was-near-the-center-of-the-milky-way/.

227 Lee Strobel, *The Case for a Creator: A Journalist Investigates Scientific Evidence That Points toward God* (Grand Rapids, MI: Zondervan, 2004),171.

228 Heeren, *Show Me God*, 43.

astronomer Donald Brownlee conclude in their book *Rare Earth*, that "not only intelligent life, but even the simplest of animal life, is exceeding rare in our galaxy and in the universe."[229] Biblically, we know that earth was created for the habitation of humans created in the image of God. In fact, unlike extraterrestrials (i.e., not of this earth), humanity was even created from the earth (Genesis 2:7; cf. Psalm 104:29; Ecclesiastes 3:20). Adam is a derivative of the Hebrew word "adamah" which can be interpreted as "of the earth."[230]

> The Lord formed the man from the soil of the ground.
>
> (Genesis 2:7a NET)

The twelfth thing you should know about the UFO phenomenon is that earth is special.

In apologetics, the "anthropic principle" teaches that creation demonstrates everything has been created on earth with humanity in mind; apparently, this isn't the case anywhere else. The Bible affirms that there's something special about the earth. In Revelation 21,

229 Peter D. Ward and Donald Brownlee, *Rare Earth: Why Complex Life Is Uncommon in the Universe* (New York: Copernicus, 2003).

230 John D. Barry ed., Lazarus Wentz ed., Douglas Mangum ed., Carrie Sinclair-Wolcott ed., Rachel Klippenstein ed., Elliot Ritzema ed., and Wendy Widder ed., "Adamah," In *The Lexham Bible Dictionary* (Bellingham, WA: Lexham Press, 2016).

the Apostle John is given a glimpse into the future that affirms this concept, with reference to not only a new heaven and a new earth but that ultimately, the two (heaven and earth) will become one. John says,

> Then I saw a new heaven and a new earth, for the first heaven and the first earth had passed away, and the sea was no more. And I saw the holy city, new Jerusalem, coming down out of heaven from God, prepared as a bride adorned for her husband. And I heard a loud voice from the throne saying, "Behold, the dwelling place of God is with man. He will dwell with them, and they will be his people, and God himself will be with them as their God."
>
> (Revelation 21:1–3 ESV)

Based upon the revelation we have in the Bible, humanity and the earth have a special place in God's heart.

Wasted Space or Intelligent Design?

In the movie *Contact*, based on the book by Carl Sagan, the question is posed, "Wouldn't it be a lot of wasted space if we're the only intelligent life in the universe?"[231] Not necessarily. The vast expanse of space further dem-

---

231 Carl Sagan, *Contact* (New York: Pocket Books, 1985).

onstrates the infiniteness and creative capabilities of God. Genesis 1:14 specifically tells us that the heavenly bodies were made for "signs" and for "seasons, and for days and years," thus, among other reasons, they were placed to assist humanity with recognizing the seasons. Many of the ancient monuments served as ancient calendars or the equivalent of a farmer's almanac that aided humanity in being able to determine the times accurately for planting and harvesting. Nonetheless, Sagan's book provides us with a glimpse into the "wasted space" worldview with another scenario involving the character Ellie Arroway, an agnostic (if not atheistic) radio astronomer and minister, when she asks him, "If there is a God, why didn't he leave a calling card?" Ironically, one of the answers is right in front of her and in her telescope.[232]

God has revealed Himself to humanity in at least three ways. The quickest answer to what God is like and how He has revealed Himself is found in Jesus. What is God like? God is like Jesus because Jesus is God (Luke 2:11; Mark 14:62; John 1:1–2, 10:30). Secondly, God has revealed Himself through His Word, the Bible (2 Timothy 3:16). Thirdly, creation also serves as a "calling card".

Psalm 19 tells us, "The heavens declare the glory of God, and the sky above proclaims His handiwork" (Psalm 19:1 ESV). In effect, this verse answers both of Arroway's (i.e., Sagan's) questions. Therefore, it would

232 Ibid.

not be a "waste of space" if we were the only intelligent terrestrial life in the universe. Rather, it serves to show the magnitude of God's omnipotence and creativity. Or, perhaps, as C.S. Lewis alluded to, is the vastness a part of God's plan to quarantine sin from spreading throughout the universe and contaminating other worlds?[233]

We see the theme of God's omnipotence illustrated through the vastness of space in Isaiah, "Lift up your eyes and look to the heavens: Who created all these? He who brings out the starry host one by one and calls forth each of them by name" (Isaiah 40:26 NIV). This verse appears within a passage (Isaiah 40:21–31) that demonstrates the omnipotence and omniscience of God. The same Hebrew word used here in Isaiah for "bring out" is also utilized in Job 38:32–33, where God says to Job, "Can you *bring forth* the constellations in their seasons or lead out the Bear with its cubs? Do you know the laws of heavens?" (NIV). The point is that the vastness of the universe is a testimony of the greatness of God (i.e., He is infinite and inexhaustible), intelligent design, and the fact that He (providentially) is in control of all things—on earth *and in the heavens.*

The Fermi Paradox — "Where Is Everybody?"

One of the primary arguments put forth for the existence of ET life is the sheer weight of the numbers, i.e.,

---

233 "Religion and Rocketry - C. S. Lewis Official Site," CSLewis.Com. Accessed April 30, 2022, https://www.cslewis.com/religion-and-rocketry/.

with all of the billions of stars and millions of galaxies in what appears to be an expanding universe, there must be intelligent life out there... somewhere. "Look at all the stars! There must be life out there!" has become somewhat of a mantra. But where are they? The Fermi Paradox presents a rarely considered aspect of this premise—*Where is everybody?*

As Dennis Overbye, a science writer specializing in cosmology, said, "If life is so easy, someone from somewhere must have come calling by now."[234] Dr. Enrico Fermi, a 20th-century physicist, was one of the first to articulate the premise that if the universe is really teeming with life (as many suggest), where are they?[235] For example, if a river is teeming with salmon, shouldn't we have caught one by now?

Some within the UFO community would say that extraterrestrials have been in contact, but still, where are they? Where's the undeniable and indisputable proof? Presently, there isn't any. Therefore, based on the evidence, it isn't arrogant to think that we are the only form of intelligent biological life in the universe. Rather, it's based upon an absence of convincing evidence. The typ-

234 Dennis Overbye, "The Flip Side of Optimism About Life on Other Planets," The New York Times, 2015, https://www.nytimes.com/2015/08/04/science/space/the-flip-side-of-optimism-about-life-on-other-planets.html.

235 Charles Mudede, "Capitalism Explains Why We Haven't Made Contact With Intelligent Aliens," Exo News, 2020, https://exonews.org/tag/enrico-fermi/.

ical misrepresentation and mantra that it's arrogant to think that we are the only intelligent life in the universe really aren't so arrogant after all. Rather, there's no tangible evidence to believe in ETI. Thus, it's not arrogant but simply objective.

Besides that, the idea that life randomly evolves is also built upon false foundations. Although evolution has gained widespread acceptance, the transition of species remains a theory that has never been proven.

> Darwin had an excuse. In his day fossil finds were relatively scarce. Today, however, more than a century after his death, we have an abundance of fossils. Still, we have yet to find even one legitimate example of transition from one species to another.[236]

An old joke used by Sunday School teachers illustrates this by imagining that a scientist approaches God and says, "God, because we've now figured out how to create life, humanity no longer needs you." "Oh, is that so?" says God, "Tell Me more." "Well," says the scientist, "we can take dirt and form it into the 3D likeness of other humans, and breathe life into it, thus creating man, like you." "Well, that's very interesting. Show Me a

---

236 Hank Hanegraaff, *The Face that Demonstrates the Farce of Evolution* (Nashville, TN: Thomas Nelson, 1998), 33.

demonstration," says the Lord. The scientist opens up a container of topsoil and starts to mold the soil into the shape of a man. "No, no, that simply will not do..." interrupts God, "Get your own dirt."

Another false theory for explaining how life began on earth is that it was seeded by ETs. Although false in its foundations, this premise only kicks the can down the road without answering who created them? People can be very creative. They can take wood, paint, pen, or brush and create beautiful works of art, yet they still have to start with God's dirt, plants, animals, water, etc., meaning that at the most basic level, we still have to start with God's elements.

> In the beginning, God created the heavens and the earth.
>
> (Genesis 1:1)

Ezekiel's Wheels

One passage that's often referenced, and generally out of context, within the UFO genre is Ezekiel's wheels, and it's important to have a proper understanding of this unusual passage.

> As I looked, behold, a storm wind was coming from the north, a great cloud with fire flashing forth continually and a bright light around it,

and in its midst something like glowing metal in the midst of the fire. (...) In the midst of the living beings there was something that looked like burning coals of fire, like torches darting back and forth among the living beings. The fire was bright, and lightning was flashing from the fire. And the living being ran to and fro like bolts of lightning. Now as I look at the living beings, there was one wheel on the earth beside the living beings, for each of the four of them. The appearance of the wheels and their workmanship was like sparkling beryl, and all four of them had the same form, their appearance and workmanship being as if one wheel were within another. Whenever they moved, they moved in any of their four directions without turning as they moved. As for their rims they were lofty and awesome, and the rims of all four of them were full of eyes round about. Whenever the living beings moved, the wheels moved with them. And whenever the living beings rose from the earth, the wheels rose also.

(Ezekiel 1:4, 13–19 NASB 1995)

Initially, these "wheels within wheels" (1:16) do indeed sound like an ancient UFO report. UFO enthusiasts regularly cite Ezekiel's "wheels" as an attempt to verify their claims of extraterrestrial interventions in the course of human history. However, a closer examination of the text clearly demonstrates that Ezekiel is communicating a *vision* from God, "In the thirtieth year, on the fifth day of the fourth month, while I was among the exiles at the Kebar River, the heavens opened and I saw a divine vision" (Ezekiel 1:1 NET). Thus, this is a vision, not an extraterrestrial visitation. There are a number of basic biblical interpretation (hermeneutic) rules that are violated when it's assumed that the "wheels" of Ezekiel are spaceships. First, we must read the passage within the entirety of its context, and second, we must attempt to interpret what the biblical author is trying to communicate to his intended audience. With this in mind, we see that this passage is the inaugural of several visions.

For starters, events seen in visions are not necessarily literal but often symbolic and/or metaphorical. Zechariah saw a vision of a flying scroll (Zechariah 5:1–4) and a woman in a basket (Zechariah 1:5–8). When John is given a vision of the "Four Horsemen" (Revelation 6:1–8) and a "beast with ten horns and seven heads" (Revelation 13:1–9), it doesn't necessitate that there will actually be physical horsemen galloping across the earth or an actual monster rising out of the Mediterranean Sea. Rather, a vision is typically given in the form of a vivid metaphor for communicating a spiritual truth or forthcoming event (prophecy).

Later in Ezekiel 11:23, we read that this "throne chariot" moved out of the Jerusalem Temple, seemingly reluctantly, pausing on the Mount of Olives before completely leaving the city. Unlike the unconditional covenants that had been made with Noah, Abraham, and eventually David, the Mosaic Covenant was a conditional covenant. Upon being led out of Egypt, it becomes apparent that the Hebrews still have a lot of Egypt in them, but God seeks to dwell among them.

However, His holiness is a consuming fire and somewhat like a spiritual nuclear reactor; prior to the Messiah, humans could only get so close. Nonetheless, God made a conditional covenant with them so that they could safely dwell within His presence. Like Adam and Eve (and you and I), their purpose was to reflect God's love and compassion to all of humanity. Since God's reputation, to a small degree, hinged upon the Hebrews accurately reflecting Him, a conditional (Mosaic) covenant was made, i.e., if the Hebrews would follow these precepts, God will provide additional blessings to them, fight their battles, and dwell *among them*. Similar to a marriage, at Mount Sinai, they exchange vows and agree to the terms, effectively saying "I do," but the Hebrews don't.

It's a short honeymoon. As early as Exodus 32, they've created an idol (golden calf) and worshipped it, violating two of the clauses, i.e., "thou shall have no other gods before me" (Exodus 20:3 KJV) and "You shall not make for yourself a carved image, or any likeness of anything that is in heaven above, or that is in the earth beneath, or that is in the water under the earth. You shall not bow down to them or serve them..." (Exodus 20:4–5 ESV). Somewhat like marriage counselors, prophets are sent who, using marriage vernacular, regularly encourage and exhort them to return. God will often use covenantal marriage language in doing so:

> "But like a woman unfaithful to her husband, so you, Israel, have been **unfaithful** to me," declares the Lord.
>
> (Jeremiah 3:20 NIV, emphasis mine)

> They are unfaithful to the Lord; they give birth to **illegitimate children**.
>
> (Hosea 5:7 NIV, emphasis mine)

> But like Adam they have transgressed the **covenant**...
>
> (Hosea 6:7 ESV, emphasis mine)

> "...Return, faithless Israel," declares the Lord, "I will frown on you no longer, for I am **faithful**," declares the Lord...
>
> (Jeremiah 3:12 NIV, emphasis mine)

"Even now," declares the Lord, "**return** to Me
with all your heart..."

(Joel 2:12 NIV, emphasis mine)

But they don't return. So, after countless warnings
for not keeping the conditional Mosaic Covenant, Israel
finally experienced the repercussions of being unfaith-
ful, resulting in the diaspora of the Northern tribes and
an exile to Babylon for the Southern tribes aka Judah.
However, even during their darkest hours with the Bab-
ylonians literally at the gates, through Jeremiah, God
says, "'For I know the plans I have for you,' declares the
Lord, 'plans to prosper you and not to harm you, plans
to give you a hope and a future'" (Jeremiah 29:11 NIV).
This hope is in a new *unconditional* covenant provided by
the Messiah, Jesus, that will be written on their hearts
(cf. Jeremiah 31:31–33; Ezekiel 36:24–27). But, at the
moment, the Hebrews are on their way to exile. They've
hung their harps in the willow trees (Psalm 137:2),
meaning they have no song in their hearts. And it's during this time that Ezekiel has the vision of the wheels.
Therefore, in this case, the creatures and the wheels are
most likely representations of angels (cf. Isaiah 6:2),
who are presented as God's attendants delivering a
message for Israel from God through Ezekiel.

Among other things, the wheels are a vision to encourage Ezekiel and Judah by reminding them of God's

attribute of omnipresence. Since the Kebar River (the location of the vision) was south of Babylon and a place of prayer for the Jewish exiles, this vision would have been most appropriate to remind Israel that wherever they went, God went—even to Babylon. In Ezekiel, Chapter 10, the prophet is given a vision of God's glory departing the temple, but later in Chapter 43, he receives an encouraging vision that the glory of the Lord would one day return.

In a similar fashion, Jesus will exhort and encourage His disciples by promising, "I am with you always, even unto the end of the world" (Matthew 28:20 KJV). Without a temple to represent God's presence and favor upon them, this vision of God's ongoing presence would've been one of consolation and encouragement. This, of course, is not the sensational explanation that sells books (thanks for buying this one) but one that must be considered when discussing Ezekiel's wheels.

By the way, unconditional covenants are a lot better than conditional covenants because it means that God will uphold His promise regardless of whether we do or not. God will do all the work. In the past, His unconditional covenants included a promise never to destroy the world by a global flood again. Other examples of His unconditional covenants include promising to make a nation out of Abraham and that the Messiah, the seed of the woman, would also be a descendant of David. In an unconditional covenant, God will uphold His promise regardless of whether we are faithful or not. This is the new covenant that's presently available for forgiveness and everlasting life through Jesus (cf. Hebrews 8:6, 13a, etc.; Ephesians 2:8–9).

> And likewise the cup after they had eaten, saying, "This cup that is poured out for you is the new covenant in my blood."
>
> (Luke 22:20 ESV)

CHAPTER 10

Cosmic Rabbit Holes

"But I don't want to go among the mad people," Alice remarked. "Oh, you can't help that," said the Cat. "We're all mad here. I'm mad. You're mad." "How do you know I'm mad?" said Alice. "You must be," said the Cat, "or you wouldn't have come here."

—Lewis Carrol
Alice's Adventures in Wonderland

"Rabbit hole" as a metaphor comes from *Alice in Wonderland* for describing a path that is thought to lead towards truth. However, it's an unending tunnel with twists and turns leading to other rabbit holes that lead to yet more detours that never really end. This is most certainly the case with certain elements of the UFO phenomenon.

There are numerous claims, testimonies, and theories about UFO phenomena for which there's no way to
verify or deny. Some of the speculative themes within
this phenomenon are unprovable and presently lack
quantitative veracity. If you follow these rabbit holes far
enough, you'll find that they often end with the occult,
making it unwise to spend too much time investigating
and speculating. Whether it be grays, reptilians, crop
circles, the majestic 12, time travel, men in black, etc.,
the rabbit holes within this field are inexhaustible. Perhaps you can shed light or uncover new evidence but be
careful that you do not get lost or never return. That being said, you should at least be aware of the following
facets of the UFO phenomena.

Bob Lazar

Area 51 became a household name largely because of
Bob Lazar. Lazar, perhaps the most controversial figure within Ufology emerged on the scene in 1989 when
George Knapp, a television reporter for KLAS in Las Vegas, did a feature story on him in which he claimed that
he had been secretly contracted by the U.S. Government
to work with alien technology, specifically a crashed flying saucer that was purported to have been from the
Zeta Reticula star system and nicknamed the "sport
model" in a secret facility south of Area 51 referred to as
S-4. In UFO lore, Lazar is a celebrity, yet with rare ex-

ceptions, he has generally been very reluctant to discuss the topic further. Approximately thirty years from the Knapp interview, a new documentary, *Bob Lazar: Area 51 & Flying Saucers*, resulted in another fifteen minutes of fame and subsequent interviews, including an appearance on Joe Rogan's podcast.[237]

In his interview with Rogan, Lazar said that he'd been hired to reverse engineer the propulsion system technology of the recovered spacecraft's reactor, which had the ability to create its own antigravitational field.[238] He described it as being similar to discovering a motorcycle in the 1800s and trying to figure out how it would function. When asked by Rogan to describe the spacecraft's details, Lazar said that it was all one color, without any right angles, décor, buttons, welding points, rivets, or restroom.[239] The craft, he said, was designed for someone about three feet in height.[240] On one occasion, he said he was able to witness a very brief test flight in which another craft had temporarily emitted a blueish glow upon lift-off and silently hovered.[241] Lazar compared the "Gimbal" UFO video to what he witnessed, saying,

237 "The Joe Rogan Experience | Podcast," Spotify, 2019. https://open.spotify.com/show/4rOoJ6Egrf8K2IrywzwOMk.

238 Ibid.

239 Ibid.

240 Ibid.

241 Ibid.

The craft that I worked on, that when it's going to travel a long distance, that is how it op-
erates. It puts its belly to the target and then
brings all of the amplifiers to power, and you
know it shoots off in that direction. It doesn't
fly as it would in a science-fiction movie. It
flies with the belly, the bottom, forward (...)
No question in my mind, that's the way the
craft operated. It's the exact same propulsion
system.[242]

Jeremy Corbell, the director of *Bob Lazar, Area 51, &
Flying Saucers*, said,

In the Gimbal video, there's a mechanistic
turn against the wind without deceleration,
and so we have a craft without rotors, without
heat signatures, without plumes, without tail
fins, and certainly no tail number, moving in
a way that is counterintuitive to our aeronautics. When Bob saw it, he said it has to be a
gravity propelled craft. That it does mimic the
propulsion system, Bob Lazar described.[243]

---

242 "The Joe Rogan Experience | Podcast," 2019.

243 Ibid.

Perhaps most notably, Lazar stated that the propulsion system required element 115 to generate the gravity field for "space-time compression."[244] In 1989, element 115 wasn't a part of the periodic table. To contextualize this, it would be somewhat like the scene from the science fiction movie *Back to the Future* when Doc Brown learns that he needs to generate 1.25 gigawatts for the flux capacitor to operate, something that he says is simply impossible in 1955. Similarly, element 115 wasn't on 1989's periodic table when Lazar said it was the missing ingredient of the craft's propulsion system.[245] However, in 2003, his statements gained more credibility when a group of Russian scientists managed to create the elusive element, labeling it Moscovium, which reportedly decays in less than a second and cannot be used for any known technology.[246] Also, it's noteworthy that in 1989, Lazar used the term *Area 51* to identify the secret facility; the U.S. Government countered by saying that there was no such place.[247] However, they would admit to its existence in 2013, confirming what Lazar had said decades prior.

---

244 Ibid.

245 Ibid.

246 "Moscovium - Element Information, Properties and Uses: Periodic Table," Royal Society of Chemistry, 2022, https://www.rsc.org/periodic-table/element/115/moscovium.

247 Nick Redfern, *Secret History: Conspiracies from Ancient Aliens to the New World Order* (Detroit, MI: Visible Ink Press, 2015).

Lazar is likable, convincing, brilliant, and quite possibly crazy—like a fox. Initially, Los Alamos denied that he had ever been an employee, but the research of a Peabody award-winning Las Vegas reporter, George Knapp, was able to verify his name being listed in a phone directory for the site.[248] In addition to a very questionable educational background at MIT and a criminal record, his credibility is, however, suspect. Not surprisingly, conspiracy theorists are quick to propose that he's being intentionally discredited. Surely, that is a possibility. Another theory is that he's unwittingly being used to misdirect people through counterintelligence, i.e., a disinformation campaign. Perhaps he's telling the truth as it was presented to him.

The Roswell Incident

Like a lawyer yelling "objection," UFO enthusiasts are always quick to point to Roswell, New Mexico, as the undisputed site of a crashed flying saucer and the smoking gun for proof of ETI and a subsequent military coverup. Accounts vary, but the general narrative is that on July 3, 1947, a UFO crashed outside of Roswell that included three dead extraterrestrials thrown from the craft and one survivor who died following a failed surgery. The debris and bodies were recovered by military

248 "Government Scientists Goes Public," Accessed May 17, 2022, https://www.gravitywarpdrive.com/Government_Scientist.htm.

personnel stationed at Roswell Army Airfield and subsequently transferred to Hangar 18 at Wright-Patterson AFB.

Throughout the latter half of the twentieth century the subject of Unidentified Flying Objects (UFOs) has evoked strong opinions and emotions. For some, the belief in or study of UFOs has assumed the dimensions of a religious quest. Others remain nonbelievers or at least skeptical of the existence of alien beings and elusive vehicles which never quite seem to manifest themselves. Regardless of one's conviction, nowhere has the debate about UFOs been more spirited than over the events that unfolded near the small New Mexico city of Roswell in the summer of 1947. Popularly known as the Roswell Incident, this event has become the most celebrated UFO encounter of all time and has stimulated enthusiasts like none other. Numerous witnesses, including former military personnel and respectable members of the local community, have come forward with tales of humanoid beings, alien technologies, and government cover-ups that have caused even the most skeptical observer to pause and take notice. Inevitably these stories coming from the desert have spawned countless articles, books, films, and even museums claiming to have proof that visitors had come from outer space.[249]

It may surprise you to know that the preceding statement is not from a UFO periodical but from the U.S. Government, specifically, a report entitled *The Roswell Report, Fact vs. Fiction in the New Mexico Desert*. There is no doubt that something did indeed crash within the vicinity of Roswell in 1947. The news of a crashed flying saucer from a small-town newspaper quickly went global, resulting in Roswell becoming internationally known with scores of books and several movies. The military's explanation of the "crash" was that it was debris from a downed balloon for a top-secret military project referred to as *Project Mogul* from nearby White Sands, NM, which was a pre-U-2 attempt to spy on Soviet Russia to ascertain their nuclear capabilities. In the summer of 1947, one of these spy balloons was possibly struck down by lightning and crashed on Mac Brazel's ranch. Although some of the debris indeed looked unlike anything Brazel or any non-Project Mogul personnel had ever seen, what's almost never reported is that *some of the debris was comprised of some very recognizable*

249 Richard L. Weaver and James McAndrews, "The Roswell Report: Fact versus Fiction in the New Mexico Desert," Defense Technical Information Center, 1995, https://apps.dtic.mil/sti/citations/ADA326148.

ingredients like rubber and balsa wood.[250] If true, these are hardly the materials you'd expect to find from a purported crashed spaceship that had traversed light years through time and space.

Make no mistake; something crashed that was initially reported as a "flying disc" by the Roswell Army Air Force. The newspaper then issued a correction, followed by an awkward news briefing hosted by the Air Force. Regardless of what exactly the debris was, it was of utmost importance to them. Why would so much attention and effort be given to collecting weather balloon debris?

The plot thickened in 2015 when photographic enhancements of the document being held by General Ramey at the July 8, 1947, press conference seemed to reveal what reads either "viewing" or "victims" of the crash. In 1947 the U.S. was already in a cold war with Soviet Russia, and it was very important for the U.S. to withhold as much information as possible from the Soviets. In 1997, on the fiftieth anniversary of the Roswell Incident, the USAF released a published report, *The Roswell Report: Case Closed* (it wasn't, I might add), stating that the debris was a pre-U2 attempt to spy on the

---

250 James McAndrews, "The Roswell Report: Case Closed," 1997, https://media.defense.gov/2010/Oct/27/2001330219/-1/-1/0/AFD-101027-030.pdf; Fort Worth Star Telegram, "New Mexico Rancher's 'Flying Disc' Proves to Be Weather Balloon-Kite," July 8, 1947.

Soviet Union, code-named *Project Mogul*, that was never meant to be public knowledge.[251]

Over the years, "participants" of the Roswell Incident possibly may have confused other events in the area, such as the testing of high-altitude parachute drops with dummies from the stratosphere (*Project High Dive*) and with test pilots, *Project Excelsior*, as well as numerous other aeronautical experiments with the July 8, 1947 report. The fact that the area was being used for covert military experiments has to be taken into account when assessing Roswell. "Air Force activities which occurred over a period of many years have been consolidated and are now represented to have occurred in two or three days in July 1947," the report said.[252] The "Aliens observed in the New Mexico desert were actually anthropomorphic test dummies that were carried aloft by U.S. Air Force high-altitude balloons for scientific research."[253]

Let me clarify that I clearly understand that information from the government has proven to be suspect, but in this case, so have the credentials of some of the "crashed UFO" theory proponents, thus adding to the enigma and rabbit hole.

---

251 McAndrews, 1997.

252 Ibid.

253 Ibid.

The Roswell Incident received some fresh wind to its sails through the publication of *The Day After Roswell* by retired Colonel Philip Corso, a *New York Times* best-seller, in which he claimed to have seen an alien body from the crash and advocated that a number of technological advances occurred as a result of the reverse engineering from the crashed spacecraft.[254] These, of course, are sensational claims but unable to be verified at this time. Three of the photographs for making his case were from the Condon Report (1969), and another suspiciously looks like an old hubcap that was thrown into the air and photographed. If true, he would've violated his oath of secrecy by writing a book on the topic, which, of course, causes one to question the reliability of the content.

It is worth mentioning that it was during this season that the military was experimenting with duplicating Nazi technology, including the creation of two unsuccessful flying discs. A 2000 issue of *Popular Mechanics* reported that "Documents declassified since then point to a (...) secret project, a 40-ft 'flying saucer designed to rain nuclear destruction on the Soviet Union from 300 miles in space."[255] Since some level of secrecy is required in all levels of research and development, it's

---

254 Philip J. Corso and William J. Birnes, *The Day after Roswell* (New York: Simon & Schuster Pocket Books, 1997).

255 Jim Wilson, "America's Nuclear Flying Saucer," *Popular Mechanics*, 2000, 177 (11), 66.

reasonable to deduce that in this particular case, there's simply insufficient evidence to conclude that a vehicle from an extraterrestrial civilization crash-landed near Roswell. Without a doubt, something crashed, and the debris which was collected was of great interest to the U.S. military. Regardless of the true catalyst behind this incident, as time goes on, the witnesses die off, memories fade, and with or without validity, ETs seem to gain more favor as the culprit.

In closing, as you go down various rabbit holes in the UFO phenomenon, remember that its trails often lead toward the occult. Jesus taught that Satan is a liar (John 8:44). Therefore, whereas there may be some needles of truth in various haystacks, we must always be mindful that the devil, and those under his influence, are masters of deception. Likewise, very good-natured people can be deceived (Matthew 24:24). Proceed with caution.

CHAPTER 11

Jesus Saves Earthlings

For God so loved the world that He gave His
only Son, that whoever believes in Him should
not perish but have eternal life.

(John 3:16)

In 1543, astronomer Nicholas Copernicus published
his heliocentric model, teaching that the earth, as well
as the other planets, rotated around the sun and not
vice-versa. This was in direct opposition to the polemic
that had the Earth at the center of the solar system and
even the universe. For some, the proposal of the heliocentric model was perceived as an attack against God,
pitting Christianity against the emerging scientific
community and creating somewhat of an "us vs. them"
between the church and science, a conflict from which
we have yet to recover fully.

We should learn from the Copernican revolution and choose our battles and dogmatism wisely regarding scientific issues that are not clearly articulated in Scripture. However, what we do know is that not only was the earth created with humanity in mind but that we humans have the unique distinction of having been created in God's image. Furthermore, God desires to be in a relationship with every human, but the sin virus has quarantined us from Him. This is why Jesus came for us; to inoculate us from sin and reconcile us into a relationship with Him, including everlasting life. As a result of sin, we are separated from God. Most of us sense that there is something in life that's missing and seek to fill the void with various things, a void that can only be filled by Jesus.

There is no way we can earn or merit everlasting life, but the Good News is that God has initiated peace with us. This is why the angel of the Lord told the shepherds, "I bring you good news that will cause great joy for all the *people*. Today (...) a Savior (Rescuer) has been born ..." (Luke 2:10–11 NIV, emphasis mine). This Savior is Jesus. Since He is God, He alone has the credentials to offer forgiveness and everlasting life.

Imagine you had cancer cells in your body that were slowly but surely killing you, yet there was a medical way in which we could extract all your cancer cells and place them into Jesus. What would happen to you? You would live. But what would happen to Jesus? He would die. This is an insufficient illustration, but it provides a glimpse into why Jesus died on the cross for humanity.

You could say, even though we were guilty as charged, He paid our bail and then served the sentence for us as well, resulting in a death sentence. The truth of the matter is that all humans have a sin virus, but unlike any other, it has eternal repercussions. The Good News is that Jesus has offered to remove these "sin cells," He's paid the bail and served your sentence in order that you can have everlasting life. This is what is meant by the term "born again". You not only get a new lease on life but everlasting life. Jesus took the penalty for our sins and placed it upon Himself when He was crucified on the cross.

> God demonstrates his own love for us, in that
> while we were still sinners, Christ died for us.
> (Romans 5:8 NET)

The Good News is that because Jesus is God, He rose to life three days after being crucified, demonstrating His victory not only over sin but death. That is why to this day, Christians celebrate Easter. Therefore, if you are willing to ask Jesus to forgive you for your sins and to place your faith in Him alone for your salvation (rather than in works) or an ETC, you too can be born again. The Bible says, "For by grace you have been saved through faith. And this is not your own doing; it is the gift of God, not a result of works, so that no one can boast" (Ephesians 2:8–9 ESV). **This is the most important thing you should know.** Would you like to tell God that you are sorry for your sins and turn your life over to Him? If yes, in your own words, pray the following:

> *Dear Jesus, I know that I am a sinner. I am sorry for my sins and know that I deserve death. Please forgive me for my sins and save my soul. I believe that you died for my sins and rose from the grave. I trust you now for my salvation. Fill me with the Holy Spirit. Thank you for forgiveness and everlasting life. In Jesus' name, amen.*

Now what? Tell another Christian that you are born again. Begin to read the Bible (start with the Book of John in the New Testament). Begin to pray and seek out other Christians with whom to worship and fellowship. Find and engage with a Bible-believing church in your area. Check out the Church's website to see what they believe about the Bible and Jesus. This is typically located under a "What We Believe" tab. They should believe that the Bible is God's inspired, authoritative Word and that Jesus is God, who rose bodily from the grave after being crucified, and that He is the only way to salvation. Welcome to the family of God!

Conclusion

He determines the number of the stars; He
gives to all of them their names.

(Psalm 147:4 ESV)

By all accounts, it's safe to say that UFOs will increase
in their frequency and become more emboldened. Not
limited to UFOs, the paranormal will become the norm.
Although the proof for ETI remains deficient and lacking, many will continue to place their hope in them for
purpose and meaning in life as well as spiritual fulfillment. In some ways, we can say that the aliens have already landed... spiritually.

In the opening chapter of *The Uninvited*, Nick Pope,
who once investigated UFOs for the British Ministry of
Defense, provides a brief history showing that since the
dawn of time, humanity has been engaging with non-
human entities in various guises. Pope concludes, "I believe that all these varied accounts stem not from mass
hysteria, but from the simple fact that people have been

interacting with otherworldly beings since the dawn of time."[256] Based upon Genesis 3:1, I concur.

Among other things, the forces of darkness will continue to use UFO phenomena as a means of misleading humans away from Jesus. Whereas the forces of darkness seek to prepare the way for the world's acceptance of evil, as Christians, we've been called to prepare the world for the return and reign of Jesus. It's going to happen. Jesus will most certainly return to rule and reign with truth and grace. Regardless of the existence of ETI, humanity on earth is in need of redemption, which is only available through Christ.

It's all about God. You were created by God and in His image to be in fellowship with Him. He loves you and has had His eyes on you before you were born. He's seen the bad things that have happened to you. He knows what keeps you up at night. He's seen all that you've done, good and bad, and He loves you. The entirety of the universe, whatever it may include, all points to God and His glory. It doesn't take very long to see that God, like any artist, likes variety, but unlike anything else, He has created you in His image and to be in a relationship with Him. You've been designed to reflect Him, His ways, goodness, kindness, and love to the ends of the earth... and perhaps beyond.

---

256 Nick Pope, *The Uninvited: An Expose on the Alien Abduction Phenomenon* (Simon & Schuster, 1997), 11.

However, rather than creating a race of mindless robots, He created humanity with the freedom of choice. This necessitates the ability to make the wrong choice and reject His love and offer of forgiveness. Nevertheless, the offer to be in a relationship with Him still stands. This is why Jesus came. He came, not as an alien from a distant galaxy, but from heaven, and took on human form to pay for our sins. It's all about God and His love for you. Because He's God, Jesus alone has the credentials to offer forgiveness and everlasting life, and we have been commissioned to spread this Good News to the uttermost parts of the earth-maybe further. Carry on.

What Is the Gospel?

The Scriptures contain some good news and some bad news.

The bad news is that we have all sinned, and as a result, we are separated from God. Most of us notice this and recognize that something is missing in our lives. The Bible says, "...There is none righteous, no not one" (Romans 3:10 KJV). This means that we cannot work our way into heaven through good deeds. No matter how many good deeds we do, they are still not enough to earn everlasting life in heaven. All of the following simply will not earn everlasting life:

- Going to church
- Giving to charity
- Helping the poor
- Being a generally good person

Now for the Good News!

Since there is no way we can work our way to God, He came to us. Jesus died in our place. Romans 5:8 (NKJV) tells us, "...God demonstrates His own love toward us, in that while we were still sinners, Christ died for us." Suppose you were in a hospital and dying of an incurable disease, and someone came and offered to take the diseased cells from your body and into theirs. If that were possible, what would happen to you? To that person? You would live, and that person would die in your place. Similarly, Jesus has offered to take the sin cells that will result in a physical and spiritual death from your body into His. He took upon Himself the sin penalty that we deserved and placed it upon Himself. He died in our place. Thus, your sins have already been paid for by Jesus-this is the Good News! This is the Gospel.

And there's more good news! Three days later, Jesus rose victoriously over sin and death. Sin and death were conquered!

What Does That Mean for You?

It means that you can be saved (rescued) through faith in Christ! You need to trust exclusively in Jesus for forgiveness and everlasting life. Ephesians 2:8–9 (NKJV) says,

> For by grace you have been saved through faith, and that not of yourselves; it is the

gift of God, not of works, lest anyone should boast.

What Should You Do?

Ask Jesus to forgive you of all your sins and place your trust in Him for your forgiveness. Below is a sample prayer that you can pray. Keep in mind that it's not the prayer itself that saves you. This prayer is simply an example of telling God what you are doing.

> *Dear God, I know that I am a sinner and that my wrongs deserve to be punished. I believe that Jesus Christ died for me and rose from the grave. I trust in Jesus alone to be my Savior. Please forgive me for my sins and take me to Heaven when I die. In Jesus' name, Amen.*

Now What?

- Grow to be like Him. As a brand-new follower of Jesus, begin studying His teachings in the New Testament. I'd like to recommend that you start with the Gospel of John (the fourth book in the New Testament).
- Pray. Begin spending time each day in communication with God.
- Worship with other believers at a local Bible-believing church.

- Tell others! Let people know what Jesus has done for you.

Why Should We Believe in the Authenticity of Jesus and His Claims?

Prophecy—Jesus fulfilled documented prophecies that were recorded centuries before His earthly ministry, including His place of birth and type of death.

The Empty Tomb—Had someone been able to produce a dead body of Jesus, it would have been exhibit A that He had not risen. However, the fact that His grave was empty after being guarded by Roman soldiers and sealed with a huge boulder demonstrated His deity. He rose on the third day, just like He said He would.

Eyewitness Accounts—After the resurrection, Jesus appeared to at least 500 people. He not only appeared to them but also ate and conversed with them.

Miracles—The documentation of His miracles confirms that He was God. What kind of a person has complete power and authority over sickness, death, nature, and spiritual forces? Only God.

Transformed Lives—The disciples who had witnessed the execution of their leader went into hiding, fearing for their lives, but something happened that so transformed them that they were willing to risk everything to spread the news that He has risen. What would cause such a paradigm shift? Seeing the resurrected Jesus! Think about it—the disciples believed that the Message was worth dying for, and now, 2000 years later, people's lives are still being transformed by the forgiveness of Jesus Christ.

He Claimed to Be God—Unlike other religious and spiritual leaders, Jesus claimed to be God, the Messiah. Furthermore, He also had supernatural miracles and powers to back up the claim. See Matthew 26:63–64 and John 14:6.

A Living Lord—Christianity is a relationship, not a religion. We can have a personal relationship with Him today by seeking His forgiveness of our sins and placing our trust in Him to rescue us from our wrongs that separate us from God.

Abbreviations and Glossary

AATIP — Advanced Aerospace Threat Identification Program. A federally funded program for the investigation of UFOs and UAP that reportedly shut down in 2012.

Essential Christian Doctrine

1. The belief that the Bible is the inspired word of God.
2. The earth, universe, and humanity were created by God.
3. Jesus is God.
4. Because Jesus is God, He alone can offer forgiveness and everlasting life.
5. Jesus was born of a Virgin.
6. Jesus died on the cross as the propitiation for humanity's sins and thus salvation is by grace, not works.
7. After three days, Jesus bodily rose from the grave.

8. Jesus will one day return to rule and reign upon the earth and will judge all of humanity throughout the ages.

ESV — English Standard Version. A 2001 translation of the Bible into English.

ET — Extraterrestrial. Broadly used to describe that which has origins that are not of earth, but generally used to refer to aliens.

ETC — Extraterrestrial Civilization. A civilization of extraterrestrial cognizant beings who have their own government and organization and are capable of communication and developing technology.

ETI — Extraterrestrial Intelligence. Used to reference extraterrestrial beings, not microbes nor bacteria, who are capable of developing spaceflight, exploration, etc. (e.g., SETI).

Fundamentalist — Today, the term "fundamentalist Christian" is generally used pejoratively or to reference Christians who are exceptionally legalistic or draconian in their lifestyle. However, it was birthed out of a series of essays published in 1910–1915 in response to the liberal (what today we'd refer to as "progressive Christianity") influences upon the church. Fundamentalist as a moniker was used to clarify that its adherents believed in Essential Christian Doctrine.

MUFON— Mutual UFO Network. A non-profit organization of mostly volunteers that collects, records, and investigates UFO reports.

NET — A 2001 English translation of the Bible that was updated in 2019 and made available for free online.

NHE — Non-Human Entity. A term generally used to imply that extraterrestrials are not from another planet but from another dimension.

SETI — Search for Extraterrestrial Intelligence. Generally equated with the SETI Institute, best known for using radio telescopes to search for technologically generated sound waves and electromagnetic radiation and/or that which is the byproduct of an ETC.

TTSA — To the Stars Academy. Founded by rock musician Tom DeLonge of Blink 182 is self-described as "an independent multimedia entertainment company."

UAP — Unidentified Aerial Phenomenon. A term proposed by Nick Pope, which not only made the UFO topic more intellectually palatable for government officials but also broadened the topic beyond tangible "objects".

UFO — Unidentified Flying Object.

References

"Al Gore Talks Climate Crisis: 'This Is the Time for a Great Reset.'" 2020. *NBC News Universal: Today Show*. https://www.today.com/video/al-gore-talks-climate-crisis-this-is-the-time-for-a-great-reset-85439045592.

Alexander, John B. 2011. UFOs: *Myths, Conspiracies, and Realities*. Thomas Dunne Books. https://www.amazon.com/UFOs-Conspiracies-John-Alexander-Ph-D/dp/125000201X.

Alnor, William M. 1990. "UFO Cults Are Flourishing in New Age Circles." *Christian Research Journal*. Summer. https://christian.net/pub/resources/text/cri/cri-jrnl/web/crj0073a.html.

"Anonymous, Interviewed by the Author, Fountain Hills, March 5, 2022." 2022.

"Aurora (Spyplane)." 2022. Aircraft Wiki. 2022. https://aircraft.fandom.com/wiki/Aurora_(spyplane).

Barcella, Laura. 2022. "Heaven's Gate, 25 Years Later: Remembering Lives Lost in Cult." Peo-

ple Weekly. 2022. https://people.com/crime/
heavens-gate-cult-suicide-remembering-lives-lost/.

Barry, John D., Lazarus Wentz, Douglas Mangum,
Carrie Sinclair-Wolcott, Rachel Klippenstein, Elliot
Ritzema, and Wendy Widder. 2016a. "Adamah." In
The Lexham Bible Dictionary. Bellingham, WA: Lex-
ham Press.

———. 2016b. "Nephilim." In *The Lexham Bible Dictionary*. Bellingham, WA: Lexham Press.

Beedle, Heidi. 2019. "Colorado's Cattle Mutilation History and the Journalist Who Wouldn't Let It Go."
Colorado Springs Indy. 2019. https://www.csindy.
com/temporary_news/colorado-s-cattle-mutila-
tion-history-and-the-journalist-who-wouldn-t-
let-it-go/article_6769e632-2de0-5997-beda-9e12f-
9088bea.html.

Blumenthal, Ralph. 2017. "On the Trail of a Secret
Pentagon U.F.O. Program." The *New York Times*.
2017. https://www.nytimes.com/2017/12/18/insider/
secret-pentagon-ufo-program.html.

Blumenthal, Ralph and Leslie Kean. 2020. "No Longer
in Shadows, Pentagon's U.F.O. Unit Will Make Some
Findings Public." New York Times. 2020. https://
www.nytimes.com/2020/07/23/us/politics/penta-
gon-ufo-harry-reid-navy.html.

Bowen ed., Charles. 1968. *Flying Saucer Review - Vol. 15,
N. 6*: November-December 1969 (FSR). Flying Saucer
Service LTD.

Brewer, Bobby. 2002. "Seven Things You Should Know about UFOs." *Christian Research Institute* 25 (2). http://web.archive.org/web/20210520005553/https://www.equip.org/article/seven-things-you-should-know-about-ufos/.

Britt, Robert Roy. 2006. "Does Education Fuel Paranormal Beliefs?" NBC News Universal. 2006. https://www.nbcnews.com/id/wbna10950526.

Brochu, Jim. 1990. *Lucy in the Afternoon: An Intimate Memoir of Lucille Ball.* New York: William Morrow & Co.

Brock, Chris. 2020. "Sidebar: 'War of Worlds' Broadcast Caused Local Worry but Panic Overstated." Arts and Entertainment | Nny360.Com. 2020. http://web.archive.org/web/20220227024905/https://www.nny360.com/artsandlife/artsandentertainment/sidebar-war-of-worlds-broadcast-caused-local-worry-but-panic-overstated/article_694adb5b-2707-5501-a5e8-a16e1c73794b.html.

Brookesmith, Peter. 1995. *UFO: The Complete Sightings Catalogue.* New York: Cassell & Co.

Brownfield, Troy. 2018. "War of the Worlds: The Greatest Halloween Prank in American History." The Saturday Evening Post. 2018. https://www.saturdayeveningpost.com/2018/10/war-of-the-worlds-the-greatest-halloween-prank-in-american-history/.

Carlson, Peter. 2002. "50 Years Ago, Unidentified Flying Objects From Way Beyond the Beltway Seized the Capital's Imagination." The Washington Post. 2002. https://www.washingtonpost.com/archive/lifestyle/2002/07/21/50-years-ago-unidentified-flying-objects-from-way-beyond-the-beltway-seized-the-capitals-imagination/59f74156-51f4-4204-96df--e12be061d3f8/.

Chamberlain, Samuel and Bruce Golding. 2021. "$770B Defense Bill Includes Agency to Investigate UFOs." New York Post. 2021. https://nypost.com/2021/12/15/770b-defense-bill-includes-agency-to-investigate-ufos/.

Chung, Frank. 2022. "Russia Ukraine: UFO Believers Think Aliens Will Stop Nuclear WW3." Nation Wide News. 2022. https://www.news.com.au/technology/science/space/ufo-believers-think-aliens-will-stop-nuclear-war/news-story/133ae70c82dfb22119ed79bfbb400e36.

"CHURCH FATHERS: Divine Institutes, Book V (Lactantius)." n.d. New Advent. Accessed April 29, 2022. https://www.newadvent.org/fathers/07015.htm.

Clark, Jerome. 1998. *The UFO Book: Encyclopedia of the Extraterrestrial*. Visible Ink Press.

Clarke, Aruthor C. 1953. *Childhood's End*. Del Ray.

Clement I, Pope. 1870. "The Clementine Homilies: Clement I, Pope: Free Download, Borrow, and

Streaming: Internet Archive." In *The Clementine Homilies*. Edinburgh: T. & T. Clark. https://archive. org/details/clementinehomiliooclem.

Close, Paris. 2020. "Demi Lovato Claims She Contacted Aliens, Shares Shocking Footage." IHeart. com. 2020. https://www.iheart.com/content/2020-10-19-demi-lovato-claims-she-contacted-aliens-shares-shocking-footage/.

"CNN.Com - Transcripts." 2007. CNN Larry King Live. 2007. https://transcripts.cnn.com/show/lkl/date/2007-07-13/segment/02.

Cofield, Calla. 2015. "Stephen Hawking: Intelligent Aliens Could Destroy Humanity, But Let's Search Anyway." Space. 2015. https://www.space. com/29999-stephen-hawking-intelligent-alien-life-danger.html.

Cohen, Ariel. 2021. "What Is Behind The U.S. Navy's 'UFO' Fusion Energy Patent?" Forbes. 2021. https:// www.forbes.com/sites/arielcohen/2021/02/08/what-is-behind-the-us-navys-ufo-fusion-energy-patent/?sh=31a1ac854733.

Condon, Edward U. 1968. "Scientific Study of Unidentified Flying Objects By the University of Colorado Undercontract N. 44620-67-C with the United States Air Force." www.ncas.org.

Corr, Jeremy. 2021. "Lt. Cmdr. Alex Dietrich." GoodStory. 2021. https://goodstory.io/lt-cmdr-alex-dietrich/.

Corso, Philip J. and William J. Birnes. 1997. *The Day after Roswell*. Simon & Schuster Pocket Books.

"'Duty, Honor, Country' by General Douglas MacArthur, May 12, 1962." 2022. The Art of Manliness. 2022. https://www.artofmanliness.com/duty-honor-country-by-general-douglas-macarthur/.

Eichler, Alex. 2010. "Russian Head of State Claims Space-Alien Contact." The Atlantic. 2010. https://www.theatlantic.com/international/archive/2010/05/russian-head-of-state-claims-space-alien-contact/340920/.

Eisenhower, Laura Magdalene. n.d. "SPIRIT REALITY Blog: Sophia." United Vibrations: Wordpress. Accessed May 16, 2022. https://unitedvibrations.wordpress.com/laura-magdalene-eisenhower/.

Epstein, Kayla. 2019. "Navy Admits UFO Videos Are Real, but Would like to Stop Using 'UFO' - The Washington Post." The Washington Post. 2019. https://www.washingtonpost.com/national-security/2019/09/18/those-ufo-videos-are-real-navy-says-please-stop-saying-ufo/.

"Former Ariz. Governor Boosts UFO Claims." 2007. NBC News Universal. 2007. https://www.nbcnews.com/id/wbna17761943.

Fort Worth Star Telegram. 1947. "New Mexico Rancher's 'Flying Disc' Proves to Be Weather Balloon-Kite," July 8, 1947.

"Full Text of 'David Jacobs The UFO Controversy In America.'" 2014. Internet Archive. 2014. https://archive.org/stream/DavidJacobsTheUFOControversyInAmerica/Nick Pope - The Uninvited - An Expose of the Alien Abduction Phenomenon_djvu.txt.

Gander, Kashmira. 2015. "Former Canadian Defence Secretary Paul Hellyer Calls on Governments to Reveal UFO Information." The Independent. 2015. https://www.independent.co.uk/news/world/americas/former-canadian-defence-secretary-paul-hellyer-calls-on-governments-to-reveal-ufo-information-10190024.html.

Garber, Stephen. 1999. "Searching for Good Science: The Cancellation of NASA's SETI Program." *Journal of The British Interplanetary Society* 52: 3–12. https://history.nasa.gov/garber.pdf.

Gilgoff, Dan. 2001. "Saucers Full of Secrets Washington City Paper." Washington City Paper. 2001. https://washingtoncitypaper.com/article/260860/saucers-full-of-secrets/.

"Giorgio Tsoukalos Aliens Memes." 2022. Memes Monkey. 2022. https://www.memesmonkey.com/topic/giorgio+tsoukalos+aliens.

"Global News: Coronavirus: Trudeau Tells UN Conference That Pandemic Provided 'Opportunity for a Reset.'" 2020. YouTube. 2020. https://www.youtube.com/watch?v=n2fp0Jeyjvw.

Goldman, Paul and Adela Suliman. 2020. "Former Israeli Space Security Chief Says Extraterrestrials Exist, and Trump Knows about It." NBC News Universal. 2020. https://www.nbcnews.com/news/weird-news/former-israeli-space-security-chief-says-extraterrestrials-exist-trump-knows-n1250333.

Good, Timothy. 1988. *Above Top Secret*. New York: William Morrow Co. https://www.amazon.com/Above-Secret-Timothy-Good-1988-06-03/dp/B01FIYTAJ4/ref=tmm_hrd_swatch_0?_encoding=UTF8&qid=&sr=.

———. 1991. *Alien Liaison: The Ultimate Secret*. Arrow books.

"Government Scientists Goes Public." n.d. Accessed May 17, 2022. https://www.gravitywarpdrive.com/Government_Scientist.htm.

Greenewald, John. 2021. "America West Airlines Flight 564 UFO Case - May 25, 1995." The Black Vault Case Files. 2021. https://www.theblackvault.com/casefiles/america-west-airlines-flight-564-ufo-case/.

Greenstreet, Steven and Jackie Salo. 2021. "UFO Expert Debunks Navy Footage of Pyramid-Shaped Objects." New York Post. 2021. https://nypost.com/2021/04/21/ufo-expert-debunks-navy-footage-of-pyramid-shaped-objects/.

Haines, Gerald K. 1997. "CIA's Role in the Study of UFOs, 1947-90." E-Asia Digital Library: Oregon Digital. 1997. https://oregondigital.org/sets/easia/oregondigital:df72rt54c#page/10/mode/1up/search/truman.

Haines, Richard, K. Efishoff, D. Ledger, L. Lemke, S. Maranto, W. Puckett, T. Roe, M. Shough, and R. Uriarte. 2007. "Report by the National Aviation Reporting Center on Anomalous Phenomena (NARCAP) It Was Stated That an Incident of This Nature at a Busy Airport like O'Hare 'Constitutes a Potential Threat to Flight Safety.'" https://static1.squarespace.com/static/5cf80ff422b5a90001351e31/t/5d02ec73123 0e20001528e2c/1560472703346/NARCAP_TR-10.pdf.

Hanegraaff, Hank. 1998. *The Face That Demonstrates the Farce of Evolution*. Nashville: Thomas Nelson.

Harrison, Scott. 2017. "From the Archives: The 1942 Battle of L.A." Los Angeles Times. 2017. https://www.latimes.com/visuals/framework/la-me-fw-archives-1942-battle-la-20170221-story.html.

Haskins, Justin. 2020. "John Kerry Reveals Biden's Devotion to Radical 'Great Reset' Movement." The

Hill. 2020. https://thehill.com/opinion/energy-environment/528482-john-kerry-reveals-bidens-devotion-to-radical-great-reset-movement/.

Hastings, Robert L. 2008. *UFOs and Nukes: Extraordinary Encounters at Nuclear Weapons Sites.* AuthorHouse.

Heeren, Fred. 2000. *Show Me God: What the Message from Space Is Telling Us about God.* Wheeling, IL: Day Star Publications.

———. 2002. "Home Alone in the Universe?" First Things. 2002. https://www.firstthings.com/article/2002/03/home-alone-in-the-universe-36.

Howe, Linda Moulton. 1980. *A Strange Harvest* (TV Movie 1980) - IMDb. https://www.imdb.com/title/tt6362274/.

Howell, Elizabeth. 2017. "Eugene Cernan: Last Man on the Moon." Space. 2017. https://www.space.com/20790-eugene-cernan-astronaut-biography.html.

Hsu, Jeremy. 2009. "Battlefield Blimp Tracks Low-Flying Cruise Missiles." Popular Science. 2009. https://www.popsci.com/military-aviation-amp-space/article/2009-08/battlefield-blimp-tracks-ground-hugging-cruise-missiles/.

Huang, Mary. 2010. "UFO in China's Skies Prompts Investigation." ABC News. 2010. https://abcnews.go.com/International/ufo-

china-closes-airport-prompts-investigation/
story?id=11159531.

"Hurd, Shane, Interview with the Author, Fountain
Hills, AZ, March 19, 2022." 2022.

Hynek, J. Allen (Joseph Allen), Philip J. Klass, and
Jacques Vallee. 1976. *The Edge of Reality: A Progress Report on Unidentified Flying Objects*. Chicago, IL: Henry
Regnery Co.

Interview with the Author. 2022. "Pope, Nick." Tucson,
Arizona.

Irenaeus, Saint, Bishop of Lyon. 1920. *The Demonstration of the Apostolic Preaching, Translated from
the Armenian with Introduction and Notes by J. Armitage Robinson - Internet Archive. Open Library.*
London: S.P.C.K. http://link.archive.org/portal/
The-demonstration-of-the-Apostolic-preaching/
l357e9BHcCA/.

"It's Time to Resolve the Roswell Mystery of 1947 | Editorials." 2022. Roswell Daily Record. 2022. https://
www.rdrnews.com/opinion/editorials/it-s-time-
to-resolve-the-roswell-mystery-of-1947/article_cb-
da24c2-02f5-5c0d-a0c7-7916ffe76492.html.

Jacobs, David Michael. 1992. *Secret Life: Firsthand Accounts of UFO Abductions*. New York: Atria; Reprint
edition (April 16, 1993).

———. 1999. *The Threat: Revealing the Secret Alien Agenda*.
New York: Simon & Schustser.

———. 2015. *Walking Among Us: The Alien Plan to Control Humanity.* New York: Disinformation Books.

"JAL Pilot's UFO Story Surfaces after 20 Years." n.d. UFO Casebook Files. Accessed April 22, 2022. https://www.ufocasebook.com/jal1628surfaces.html.

Jaroff, Leon. 1996. "Listening for Aliens." Time USA, LLC. 1996. https://content.time.com/time/subscriber/article/0,33009,984075,00.html.

Kean, Leslie. 2010. *UFOs: Generals, Pilots, and Government Officials Go on the Record.* New York: Rivers Press.

Keel, John A. 1970. *Operation Trojan Horse: The Classic Breakthrough Study of UFOs.* New York: Anomalist Books.

Keyhoe, Donald E. (Donald Edward). 1950, reprint 2004. *The Flying Saucers Are Real.* Cosimo Classics.

Kennedy, Courtney and Arnold Lau. 2021. "Most Americans Believe Life on Other Planets Exists." Pew Research Center. 2021. https://www.pewresearch.org/fact-tank/2021/06/30/most-americans-believe-in-intelligent-life-beyond-earth-few-see-ufos-as-a-major-national-security-threat/.

Kidner, Derek. 1967. *Genesis: An Introduction and Commentary.* Leicester: Inter-Varsity Press. https://www.amazon.com/Genesis-Introduction-Commentary-Derek-Kidner/dp/B000O20A36.

Kinick, Jacquelyn. 2021. "Navy Pilots Recall 'Unsettling' 2004 UAP Sighting." 60 Minutes - CBS News. 2021. https://www.cbsnews.com/news/navy-ufo-sighting-60-minutes-2021-05-16/.

Kitei, Lynne D. 2004. *The Phoenix Lights: A Skeptic's Discovery That We Are Not Alone*. Charlottesville, VA: Hampton Roads Publishing Co.

Klein, Ezra. 2021. "Opinion | Barack Obama Interview: Joe Biden Is 'Finishing the Job.'" The New York Times. 2021. https://www.nytimes.com/2021/06/01/opinion/ezra-klein-podcast-barack-obama.html.

Kress, Kenneth A. 1999. "Full Text of 'Parapsychology In Intelligence: A Personal Review and Conclusions' - Original Report 1977." *Journal of Scientific Exploration* 13 (1). https://archive.org/stream/Parapsychology-InIntelligence/Parapsychology-in-Intelligence_djvu.txt.

Kube, Courtney and Adam Edelman. 2021. "UFO Report: Government Can't Explain 143 of 144 Mysterious Flying Objects, Blames Limited Data." NBC News Universal. 2021. https://www.nbcnews.com/politics/politics-news/ufo-report-government-can-t-explain-143-144-mysterious-flying-n1272390.

Lagerfeld, Nathalie. 2016. "How an Alien Autopsy Hoax Captured the World's Imagination for a Decade." Time. 2016. https://time.com/4376871/alien-autopsy-hoax-history/.

"Larry King Now: Season 7, Episode 72 - Rotten Tomatoes." 2019. https://www.rottentomatoes.com/tv/larry_king_now/s07/e72.

Lee, Jane J. 2015. "China's Floating City and The Science of Mirages." National Geographic. 2015. https://www.nationalgeographic.com/science/article/151020-city-sky-china-mirage-fata-morgana-weather-atmosphere.

Lewis, C. S. (Clive Staples). 2005. "The Last Battle." Harper Collins Publishers (first published September 4th, 1956).

Lewis, James R. 1995. *The Gods Have Landed: New Religions from Other Worlds*. State University of New York Press.

Longenecker, Dwight and David Gustafson. 2003. *Mary: A Catholic-Evangelical Debate*. Gracewing Publishing.

Lowell, Percival. 1906. *Mars and Its Canals*. New York: The Macmillian Company.

Lucas, Greg. n.d. "The Battle of Los Angeles." California State Library. Accessed April 20, 2022. https://cal170.library.ca.gov/february-24-1942-the-battle-of-los-angeles-2/.

Mack, John E. 1994a. *Abduction: Human Encounters with Aliens*. Scribner's.

———. 2009. *Abduction: Human Encounters with Aliens*. New York: Scribner.

Major Boggs. 1949. "Project Grudge: Secrets Declassified." https://www.secretsdeclassified.
af.mil/Portals/67/documents/AFD-110719-005.
pdf?ver=2016-07-19-142520-690.

Maksimovska, Elizabeta. 2019. "What If Earth Was
Near the Center of the Milky Way?" INSH World.
2019. https://insh.world/science/what-if-earth-
was-near-the-center-of-the-milky-way/.

"Man's Last Footsteps On The Moon Historical Marker." 2022. The Historical Marker Database. 2022.
https://www.hmdb.org/m.asp?m=62881.

Marciniak, Barbara and Tera Thomas. 1992. *Bringers of
the Dawn: Teachings from the Pleiadians.* Bear & Co.

Martyr, Justin. n.d. "The Second Apology of Justin."
Justin Martyr, Second Apology. Accessed April 29,
2022. https://www.biblestudytools.com/history/
early-church-fathers/ante-nicene/vol-1-apostolic-
with-justin-martyr-irenaeus/justin-martyr/second-
apology-of-justin.html.

McAndrews, James. 1997. "The Roswell Report:
Case Closed." https://media.defense.gov/2010/
Oct/27/2001330219/-1/-1/0/AFD-101027-030.pdf.

McClaim, Sierra Dawn. 2021. "Mysterious Cattle Mutilations Continue in Central and Eastern Oregon."
Capital Press. 2021. https://www.capitalpress.com/
ag_sectors/livestock/mysterious-cattle-mutila-

tions-continue-in-central-and-eastern-oregon/
article_47e16326-0537-11ec-a50e-c7abb8e5e93e.html.

Media, Sun. 2020. "EDITORIAL: Trudeau Sees Pandemic as an 'Opportunity.'" Toronto Sun. 2020. https://torontosun.com/opinion/editorials/editorial-trudeau-sees-pandemic-as-an-opportunity.

"Medjugorje 41 Years of Apparitions." n.d. Foundation Marypages. Accessed May 16, 2022. https://www.marypages.com/medjugorje-(bosnia-and-herzegovina)-en.html.

"Mexico City UFO." n.d. Unsolved Mysteries Wiki. Accessed April 20, 2022. https://unsolvedmysteries.fandom.com/wiki/Mexico_City_UFO.

Moon, Troy. 2017. "Gulf Breeze UFO Sightings: 30 Years Later, Public Still Divided." *Pensacola News Journal*. 2017. https://www.pnj.com/story/news/2017/12/10/gulf-breeze-ufo-sightings-30-years-public-divided/915397001/.

"Moscovium - Element Information, Properties and Uses: Periodic Table." 2022. Royal Society of Chemistry. 2022. https://www.rsc.org/periodic-table/element/115/moscovium.

Mudede, Charles. 2020. "Capitalism Explains Why We Haven't Made Contact With Intelligent Aliens." Exo News. 2020. https://exonews.org/tag/enrico-fermi/.

Myers, Craig R. 2006. *War of the Words: The True but Strange Story of the Gulf Breeze UFO*. Xlibris.

Mystery Wire. 2021. "UFO Report: Government Unable to Explain Aerial Phenomena in Long-Awaited Document." CBS42:Nexstar Media Inc. 2021. https://www.cbs42.com/news/u-s-world/ufo-report-published-by-the-office-of-the-director-of-national-intelligence/.

O'Brien, Christopher. 2014. *Stalking the Herd: Unraveling the Cattle Mutilation Mystery*. Kempton: IL: Adventures Unlimited Press.

O'Toole, Thomas. 1977. "UFO Over Georgia? Jimmy Logged One." The Washington Post. 1977. https://www.washingtonpost.com/archive/politics/1977/04/30/ufo-over-georgia-jimmy-logged-one/080ef1c3-6ff3-41a9-a1e4-a37c54b5cbca/.

Olson, Tyler. 2022. "Congress Holds Historic Public UFO Hearing, as Military Struggles to Understand 'Mystery' Flying Phenomena." FOX News Network, LLC. 2022. https://www.foxnews.com/politics/house-intelligence-committee-ufo-hearing.

"OPERATION SNOWBIRD and The Phoenix Lights Flare Drop | 20th Anniversary of The Phoenix Lights | Interview with Kenny Young 8-5-1997." 2017. The UFO Chronicles. 2017. https://www.theufochronicles.com/2017/03/operation-snowbird-phoenix-lights.html.

Overbye, Dennis. 2015. "The Flip Side of Optimism About Life on Other Planets." The New York Times.

2015. https://www.nytimes.com/2015/08/04/science/space/the-flip-side-of-optimism-about-life-on-other-planets.html.

"Paraphysical." 2022. In *Merriam-Webster Online Dictionary*. Merriam-Webster, Incorporated. https://www.merriam-webster.com/dictionary/paraphysical.

"Paul Fredricks (Pastor), Interview on the Phoenix Lights with the Author, January 29, 2022." 2022.

Pitterson, Ryan. 2021. The Final Nephilim. New York: Days of Noe Publishing.

Pope, Nick. 1997. *The Uninvited: An Exposé of the Alien Abduction Phenomenon*. Simon & Schuster.

"President Clinton Statement Regarding Mars Meteorite Discovery." 1996. The White House Office of the Press Secretary. 1996. https://www2.jpl.nasa.gov/snc/clinton.html/%22.

"Prince Charles Says We Need a Global Marshall Plan to Save the Environment." 2020. World Economic Forum. 2020. https://www.weforum.org/videos/prince-charles-says-we-need-a-global-marshall-plan-to-save-the-environment.

"Project BLUE BOOK - Unidentified Flying Objects." 2020. National Archives: Military Records. 2020. https://www.archives.gov/research/military/airforce/ufos?_ga=2.168296481.1048005295.1651673900-559772480.1651673900#usafac.

"Quote by Francis Schaeffer." 2022. A-Z Quotes. 2022. https://www.azquotes.com/quote/467317.

"Quote by H. G. Wells, Book *War of the Worlds*, 1898." 2022. Quotepark. 2022. https://quotepark.com/quotes/1920484-h-g-wells-yet-across-the-gulf-of-space-minds-that-are-to-o/.

"Quote by Lewis Carroll." 2021. Quotepark. 2021. https://quotepark.com/quotes/1282040-lewis-carroll-but-i-dont-want-to-go-among-mad-people-alice-re/.

Randall Tan and David A. DeSilva. 2009. "Sperm."Logos Bible Software. *The Lexham Greek-English Interlinear Septaugint: Rahlfs Edition*. Logos Bible Software. Ge 3:15.

Raymond, Adam K. 2020. "UFO Report: Pentagon Has 'Off-World Vehicles' Not From Earth." New York Intelligencer. 2020. https://nymag.com/intelligencer/2020/07/ufo-report-pentagon-has-off-world-vehicles-not-from-earth.html.

Reagan, Ronald. 1986. "Address by President Ronald Reagan to the UN General Assembly." U.S. Department of State. 1986. https://2009-2017.state.gov/p/io/potusunga/207357.htm.

Redfern, Nicholas. 2010. Final Events and the Secret Government Group on Demonic UFOs and the Afterlife. San Antonio, TX: Anomalist Books.

Redfern, Nick. 2015. *Secret History: Conspiracies from Ancient Aliens to the New World Order.* Detroit, MI: Visible Ink Press.

———. 2016. "UFOs: Extraterrestrial? Probably Not." Mysterious Universe. 2016. https://mysteriousuniverse.org/2016/04/ufos-extraterrestrial-probably-not/.

Reich, Aaron. 2020. "Former Israeli Space Security Chief Says Aliens Exist, Humanity Not Ready." The *Jerusalem Post.* 2020. https://www.jpost.com/omg/former-israeli-space-security-chief-says-aliens-exist-humanity-not-ready-651405.

"Religion and Rocketry." n.d. C.S. Lewis.com. Accessed April 30, 2022. https://www.cslewis.com/religion-and-rocketry/.

Rennenkampff, Marik von. 2022. "UFOs, the Channel Islands and the Navy's 'Drone Swarm' Mystery." MSN: The Hill. 2022. https://thehill.com/opinion/national-security/588223-ufos-the-channel-islands-and-the-navys-drone-swarm-mystery/.

Revkin, Andrew C. 2006. "NASA's Goals Delete Mention of Home Planet." New York Times. 2006. https://www.nytimes.com/2006/07/22/science/22nasa.html.

Ridenour, Fritz and Robert Williams. 2001. *So What's the Differenc : A Look at the 20 Worldviews, Faiths and Religions and How They Compare to Christianity.* Ventura, CA: Bethany House.

Rogers, James and Chris Ciaccia. 2020. "With Pentagon UFO Unit in the Spotlight, Report Mentions 'off-World Vehicles Not Made on This Earth.'" Tucker Carlson Tonight: Fox News. 2020. https://www.foxnews.com/science/pentagon-ufo-unit-spotlight-vehicles-earth.

Romero, Frances. 2011. "Mexico City - 6 UFO Hot Spots Around the World." Time. 2011. http://content.time.com/time/specials/packages/article/0,28804,2072479_2072478_2072471,00.html.

Ronk, Liz. 2022. "Marilyn Monroe: LIFE Magazine Covers, 1952-1962." Life. 2022. https://www.life.com/people/marilyn-monroe-life-magazine-covers-photos/.

Rose, Joseph. 2016. "UFOs, Mutilated Cows and Oregon: What's the Link? (Photos) - Oregonlive. Com." The Oregonian: Oregon Live. 2016. https://www.oregonlive.com/entertainment/2016/02/ufo_cow_mutilations_oregon_no.html.

Ross, Hugh, Kenneth Samples, and Mark Clark. 2002. *Lights in the Sky & Little Green Men.* Colorado Springs: CO: NavPress Publishing Group.

Saad, Lydia. 2021. "Do Americans Believe in UFOs?" Gallup, Inc. 2021. https://news.gallup.com/poll/350096/americans-believe-ufos.aspx.

Sagan, Carl. 1985. *Contact.* New York: Pocket Books.

Sagan, Carl and Thornton; American Association for the Advancement of Science Page. 1996. *UFOs: A Scientific Debate.* New York City: Barnes Noble Books.

Salisbury, David F. 1998. "Scientific Panel Concludes Some UFO Evidence Worthy of Study (6/98)." Stanford News Service. 1998. https://news.stanford.edu/pr/98/980629ufostudy.html.

Samuelson, Arielle. 2019. "NASA Designing Shapeshifting Robots for Saturn's Moons." Webpage of NASA Jet Propulsion Laboratory. 2019. https://www.jpl.nasa.gov/news/nasa-designing-shapeshifting-robots-for-saturns-moons.

Schwab, Klaus. 2020. "Now Is the Time for a 'Great Reset' of Capitalism." World Economic Forum. 2020. https://www.weforum.org/agenda/2020/06/now-is-the-time-for-a-great-reset/.

Scigliuzzo, Davide, Josh Saul, Shannon D. Harrington, Claire Boston, and Demetrios Pogkas. 2020. "Bankrupt Companies 2020: Businesses That Went Bust Because of Covid, Guitar Center to Francesca's." Bloomberg L.P. 2020. https://www.bloomberg.com/graphics/2020-us-bankruptcies-coronavirus/.

Shakespeare, William. n.d. "Hamlet Act 1 Scene 5." Genius. Accessed April 29, 2022. https://genius.com/William-shakespeare-hamlet-act-1-scene-5-annotated.

Shostak, Seth. 2021. "Project Ozma." SETI Institue. 2021. https://www.seti.org/project-ozma.

Smith, Jeff. 2013. "Thinking Flashes in the Sky (Part 1)." San Diego Reader. 2013. https:// www.sandiegoreader.com/news/2013/sep/11/ unforgettable-thinking-flashes-sky-part-1/.

Smith, Ryan. 2013. "O'Hare UFO Sighting in 2006 One of the Most Famous Reported." Chicago Tribune. 2013. https://www.chicagotribune.com/redeye/ct-redeye-xpm-2013-03-20-37880251-story.html.

Sparks, Hannah. 2021. "NASA Hired 24 Theologians to Study Reaction to Aliens: Book." New York Post. 2021. https://nypost.com/2021/12/27/nasa-hired-24-theologians-to-study-reaction-to-aliens-book/.

Stearman, Gary. 2014. *Time Travelers of the Bible: How Hebrew Prophets Shattered the Barriers of Time-Space.* Oklahoma City: Blessed Hope Publishing.

Steiger, Brad. 1988. *The Fellowship: Spiritual Contact between Humans and Outer Space Beings.* Doubleday.

Strieber, Whitley. 1988. *Transformation: The Breakthrough.* New York: William Morrow & Co.

Strieber, Whitney and James Kunetka. 1987. *Communion: A True Story.* Beech Tree Books.

Strobel, Lee. 2004. *The Case for a Creator: A Journalist Investigates Scientific Evidence That Points Toward God.* Grand Rapids, MI: Zondervan.

Sweetman, Bill. 2006. "The Top-Secret Warplanes of Area 51." *Popular Science*. 2006. https://www.popsci.com/military-aviation-space/article/2006-10/top-secret-warplanes-area-51/.

Szymanski, Mike. 2012. "Eisenhower Great-Granddaughter Discusses Time Travel, Mars and ETs." Patch Media. 2012. https://patch.com/california/studiocity/eisenhower-great-granddaughter-discusses-time-travel-5503567164.

Tan, Randall and David A. DeSilva. 2009. "Sperm." In *A Dictionary of Biblical Languages w/ Semantic Domains: Hebrew (OT)*. Lexham Press.

Tertullian. 1889. *Tertullian: The Apology, Translated by Wm. Reeve, (1709 Reprinted 1889)*. Griffith, Farran, Okeden & Welsh Newberry House. https://www.tertullian.org/articles/reeve_apology.htm.

"The 5th Dimension - Aquarius / Let The Sunshine In Lyrics." 2022. AZLyrics. 2022. https://www.azlyrics.com/lyrics/5thdimension/aquariusletthesunshinein.html.

The Editors of Publications International, Ltd. 2022. "Ronald Reagan Sees a UFO." How Stuff Works. 2022. https://science.howstuffworks.com/space/aliens-ufos/ronald-reagan-ufo.htm.

"The Great Reset." 2022. World Economic Forum. 2022. https://www.weforum.org/great-reset.

"The Joe Rogan Experience | Podcast." 2019.
    Spotify. 2019. https://open.spotify.com/
    show/4rOoJ6Egrf8K2IrywzwOMk.

The Office of the Director of National Intelligence.
    2021. "Preliminary Assessment: Unidentified Aerial
    Phenomena."

Thompson, Dorothy. 1938. "Mr. Welles and Mass
    Delusion." New York Herald Tribune. 1938. https://
    rwoconne.github.io/rwoclass/astr1210/welles-and-
    mass-delusion-DThompson-1938.html.

"Travis Walton, Interviewed by the Author, Snowflake,
    AZ, March 28, 2022." 2022.

Tuella, Timothy Green. Beckley, Commander Ashtar,
    and Ashtar Command. 1993. *Project World Evacuation:
    UFOs to Assist in the "Great Exodus" of Human Souls off
    This Planet.* Inner Light Publications.

Vallee, Jacques. 2008. *Messengers of Deception: UFO Con-
    tacts and Cults.* Daily Grail Publishing.

Vallee, Jacques and Philip J. Klass. 1967. *Edge of Reality:
    A.* Chicago, IL: Henry Regnery Co.

Vazquez, Galan. 2020. "Terror in the Air: Mission Shoot
    Down the UFO." Medium. 2020. https://caballode-
    troy.medium.com/terror-in-the-air-mission-shoot-
    down-the-ufo-cfd367b07563.

Vicens, AJ. 2016. "Hillary Clinton Is Serious
    About UFOs." Mother Jones. 2016. https://

www.motherjones.com/politics/2016/03/ hillary-clinton-and-ufo-thing-just-wont-go-away/.

"Video of UFOs Taken by U.S. Warship Called Best 'World Has Ever Seen.'" 2021. Toronto Sun. 2021. https://torontosun.com/news/weird/video-of-ufos-taken-by-u-s-warship-called-best-world-has-ever-seen.

Walton, Travis. 1978. *The Walton Experience*. New York: Berkley Pub. Corp.

Ward, Peter D and Donald Brownlee. 2003. *Rare Earth: Why Complex Life Is Uncommon in the Universe.* New York: Copernicus. https://doi.org/10.1063/1.1325239.

Warren, Frank. 2006. "Ford's UFO Legacy: Unapproving of The Air Force's Explanation He Requests Congressional Investigation." The UFO Chronicles. 2006. https://www.theufochronicles.com/2006/12/fords-ufo-legacy-unapproving-of-air.html.

"Watch USS Nimitz 'Tic Tac' UFO: Declassified Video Clip." 2022. History Channel: A&E Television Networks, LLC. 2022. https://www.history.com/videos/uss-nimitz-tic-tac-ufo-declassified-video.

Watson, Eleanor. 2021. "Pentagon Confirms Authenticity of Videos Showing Unidentified Flying Objects." CBS News. 2021. https://www.cbsnews.com/news/ufo-video-authenticity-pentagon/.

Weaver, Richard L. and James McAndrews. 1995. "The Roswell Report: Fact versus Fiction in the New Mex-

ico Desert." Defense Technical Information Center.
1995. https://apps.dtic.mil/sti/citations/ADA326148.
"What Happened at the Rendelsham Forest Incident,
Britain's Answer to Roswell?" 2022. History Chan-
nel: A&E Television Networks, LLC. 2022. https://
www.history.co.uk/articles/what-happened-at-the-
rendelsham-forest-incident-britain-s-answer-to-
roswell.
Wheeler, Dave. 2012. "Astronaut Gordon Cooper Talks
About UFO Sightings." 96.1 The Eagle, Townsquare
Media, Inc. 2012. https://961theeagle.com/astro-
naut-gordon-cooper-talks-about-ufo-sightings/.
Wikipedia Contributors. 2022a. "Alaska Airlines
Flight 261." Wikipedia, The Free Encyclope-
dia. 2022. https://en.wikipedia.org/wiki/
Alaska_Airlines_Flight_261.
———. 2022b. "Alien Autopsy." Wikipedia, The Free
Encyclopedia. 2022. https://en.wikipedia.org/wiki/
Alien_autopsy.
———. 2022c. "Aurora (Aircraft)." Wikipedia, The Free
Encyclopedia. 2022. https://en.wikipedia.org/wiki/
Aurora_(aircraft).
———. 2022d. "Barney and Betty Hill." Wikipedia, The
Free Encyclopedia. 2022. https://en.wikipedia.org/
wiki/Barney_and_Betty_Hill.

———. 2022e. "Battle of Los Angeles." Wikipedia, The Free Encyclopedia. 2022. https://en.wikipedia.org/wiki/Battle_of_Los_Angeles.

———. 2022g. "Frankenstein (1931 Film)." Wikipedia, The Free Encyclopedia. 2022. https://en.wikipedia.org/wiki/Frankenstein_(1931_film).

———. 2022h. "Gulf Breeze UFO Incident." Wikipedia, The Free Encyclopedia. 2022. https://en.wikipedia.org/wiki/Gulf_Breeze_UFO_incident.

———. 2022i. "To Serve Man (The Twilight Zone) - Wikipedia." Wikipedia, The Free Encyclopedia. 2022. https://en.wikipedia.org/wiki/To_Serve_Man_(The_Twilight_Zone).

———. 2022j. "Travis Walton UFO Incident." Wikipedia, The Free Encyclopedia. 2022. https://en.wikipedia.org/wiki/Travis_Walton_UFO_incident.

Willson, Jim. 1999. "Alien World: Startling Discoveries by NASA Scientists Suggest the Universe May Be Teeming with Exotic Life-Forms." *Popular Mechanics* 176 (7): 66.

Wilson, Clifford. 1976. *The Chariots Still Crash*. New York: Signet.

Wilson, Jim. 2000. "America's Nuclear Flying Saucer." *Popular Mechanics* 177 (11): 66.

Withnall, Adam. 2014. "Pope Francis Says He Would Baptise Aliens: 'Who Are We to Close Doors?'" *The*

Independent. 2014. https://www.independent.co.uk/
news/world/europe/pope-francis-says-he-would-
baptise-aliens-9360632.html.

Writers, Community History. 2018. "No Mention of
Satanic Cults – or UFOs – in CBI Report." *The Fort
Morgan Times*. 2018. https://www.fortmorgantimes.
com/2018/11/05/no-mention-of-satanic-cults-or-
ufos-in-cbi-report/.

Yenne, Bill. 2014. *Area 51 – Black Jets: A History of the Aircraft Developed at Groom Lake, America's Secret Aviation
Base*. Minneapolis: Zenith Press.

Yonge (Translator), Charles Duke. 1993. *The Works of
Philo: Complete and Unabridged*. Hendrickson Pub.

About the Author

Dr. Bobby Brewer (Doctorate of Ministry, Phoenix Seminary, Master of Divinity, Liberty Baptist Theological Seminary) has served on the pastoral staff of several evangelical Bible churches in the Phoenix area and co-hosted a radio talk show for fifteen years. He is the author of *Postmodernism: What You Should Know and Do About It* and served as a contributor for a layman's commentary on the Book of Ecclesiastes.

See sermonmessages.com for more.

You alone *are* the LORD; You have made heaven, The heaven of heavens, with all their host, The earth and everything on it, The seas and all that is in them, And You preserve them all. The host of heaven worships You.

(Nehemiah 9:6 NKJV)